Joyful Generosity

Responding to God's Grace

Steve Swartz

Copyright © 2019 Steve Swartz
Joyful Generosity:
Responding to God's Grace

All rights reserved. No portion of this book may be reproduced in any form without the written permission of the publisher except for brief excerpts quoted in critical reviews.

Published by:
Kress Biblical Resources
www.kressbiblical.com

Unless otherwise indicated, Scripture quotations are from The Holy Bible, English Standard Version (ESV), copyright © 2001 by Crossway Bibles, a publishing ministry of Good News Publishers. Used by permission. All rights reserved.

ISBN: 978-1-934952-46-7

To the faithful saints of Grace Bible Church of Bakersfield. When presented with the opportunity to do something extraordinarily generous, you went above and beyond to amazing heights. Your generosity to kingdom tasks shows your appreciation of salvation by grace, your love for Christ, and your care for His Church. May you be so faithful until Christ returns with His reward in hand.

Many thanks also to Heather Olewiler who faithfully and <u>quickly</u> transformed my sermon notes into this book. And thanks to the whole Steadfast In The Faith team who got behind this project for the sake of Christ's church.

Contents

Preface: Why This Book? 1

Chapter 1: Why Does the Subject of Giving Make Me Squirm? 5

Chapter 2: Give Because of God's Ownership 12

Chapter 3: Give Because of God's Grace 21

Chapter 4: Give Because of God's Provision 33

Chapter 5: Give Because of God's Church 43

Chapter 6: Give Because of God's Reward 56

Chapter 7: Give Because of God's Glory 70

Chapter 8: Give Because of God's Kingdom 86

Appendix: Our Rationale for a Capital Campaign 100

Endnotes 105

Preface: Why This Book?

This book is *not* about money. More about that in a moment. This book arose out of a short series of messages I preached as part of a capital campaign to raise funds for a needed church facility. Our leadership worked hard to establish the gospel priorities of any such campaign. We had already held a church-wide banquet during which we laid out some of the reasons we prayerfully believed we needed to more aggressively pursue a permanent church home. Our church is a relatively new congregation and as such, had never been through a giving project of this scope and size. In our case, our current facility (at the time of this writing) was leased with a high monthly rent. We could not in good conscience simply perpetually throw God's money away with no plan for better use of His funds in the future. I'll share some of our other reasons in the appendix, but first I wanted to explain the reasoning for that sermon series (and for this book).

To be clear, our facility was not a *bad* facility. The facility we were using (as of this writing) had a wonderful and cherished history with many church members donating countless hours of labor to build (inside a tilt-up prefabricated building shell). The Lord used this facility as a meeting place for the church and for the gospel of Christ to be proclaimed. We baptized many new believers in this facility and built years of precious memories of the Lord's faithfulness. But like anything good, sometimes there is a right time to begin moving forward. By God's grace, we had outgrown this facility and were cramped in our ability to pursue meaningful ministry in various ways.

The subject of money makes people nervous. Money is such an integral part of our lives and the means by which we have food, a place to live, transportation, and all the things we need (or *think* we need) to exist in this world. So, when anyone starts poking at it, *people get tense.* To be quite honest, *I get tense also*, because as a pastor, my human nature wants to just preach that which *relieves* anxiety, not *causes* it! But sometimes to *relieve* anxiety, you must face the very thing that made you anxious in the first place.

My goal was to slowly build a theology of giving (certainly not comprehensive) to demonstrate that giving is simply—no more and no less—one of many areas of life which serve as the barometer for the state of your heart. A truly born-again Christian has a heart to give *because he has a heart of obedience*. The admonitions in the Bible (particularly the New Testament) are no different than the exhortations concerning marriage, raising children, the priorities of men and women, the church, prayer, relationships, and all the other parts of life which we offer to the Lord as now belonging to *Him*.

As a teacher and preacher of God's Word, I believe it is my duty to present a viable argument from Scripture for any area of life in which I am calling people to change and realign. It isn't enough to just say, "Give because the Bible says so," or "Be a good husband because the Bible says so." I am called to present the detailed argument or case from Scripture, so that the congregant can clearly see that these things are commanded by the Lord God and not just the result of the pastor's whims or fancies. Nor is it enough to just throw around a verse or two. A more comprehensive case must be made, particularly if I am calling people to a lifestyle which costs them sacrificially for the sake of Christ.

Thus, it was my hope to build an argument for giving, and not just giving toward the regular functions of the church, but toward the reasonable, larger-picture projects that the leadership of the church prayerfully embraced. There are numbers of capital campaigns a church could embark upon. For example, our church annually raises extra money for Christmas "bonuses" for the missionaries we support. We also ask an extra offering once per month for our benevolence fund which goes to help church members in dire need. In this case, we bit off a somewhat larger campaign, that of working toward a new facility.

For you who are reading this book, I said upfront that this book is *not* about money. It is first and foremost about your heart and your love for the Lord Jesus Christ. I *know* that the subject of giving is so very tender to so many of you, and that's why the entire introductory chapter exists to soothe your anxieties. But the fact remains that giving is simply one of the many areas of life with which we proclaim our love and allegiance to our Savior and Lord. If you are already skeptical, let me give you two pieces of encouragement.

First, if you will challenge yourself to read this book slowly and prayerfully, then test the arguments *against Scripture*. Don't test them against your emotions or experience; those have no authority. Test these arguments and see if they stand firm. That's all I can ask. Second, if you get through the book and *still* think preachers should mind their own business about giving, this book will make a great coaster, big enough for two coffee cups, so at least your investment wasn't a complete waste. But I hope the rationale will convince you to evaluate your heart regarding how you allocate your resources for kingdom work and for the gospel of Christ. It's all His anyway!

Steve Swartz

Chapter 1

Why Does the Subject of Giving Make Me Squirm?

There is a *big* difference between preaching a sermon on financial giving (which I have done many times) and writing a book about financial giving. The major difference is that if you walked into our church for the first time and I started preaching on giving, even if you *hated* every word I said, you would probably endure the sermon out of social politeness. Oh, you might count down the minutes until you could slip out, but you might even pick up a couple of thoughts just by passive listening. But with a *book* on giving, all you have to do is look at the cover and *never even pick it up!* So, the fact that you are even reading this paragraph makes me extremely thankful!

But that does bring up the question that we might all ask ourselves: Why does the subject of giving make me squirm? Why is it that I might want my pastor to preach on anything else *except* giving? "Pastor, let's talk about the love of God or the Ten Commandments or the Sermon on the Mount—just *spare* me the sermon on giving!"

I'd like to offer a few thoughts that may help explain this dynamic. And it is my hope that you will then venture on into the following chapters and see how the Lord would work in your own heart, because giving financially has really nothing to do with money. It has *everything* to do with the state of your heart and your love for Christ. But before I move on into the meat of the book, I'd like to share a few thoughts concerning our cultural discomfort with the topic of financial giving. Let's discuss preaching on giving, misunderstandings about giving, worship and giving, and cynicism about giving.

Preaching on Giving

Many have long observed a reflex reaction to pastors preaching on giving because of the personal nature of this topic. As a pastor, I've been told to my face, "You can preach to me about anything you want except for my money." But the mandate of preaching is clear in 2 Timothy 3:16, "All Scripture is breathed out by God and profitable for teaching, for reproof, for correction, and for training in righteousness." If something is addressed in Scripture, it is a pastor's sworn duty to preach about it. *No* part of our lives warrants being completely above any sort of accountability, because *every* part of life is addressed in Scripture!

Preaching about money *is not* really about money; it's merely a spiritual EKG to check your heart. How you think about money reveals the state of your heart, because anything you claim as yours rather than the Lord's is ultimately a potential idol in your life. The more mature and deep a believer's faith, the more he will not only tolerate sermons about giving, but also the more he will feel nourished by them. As a preaching pastor, I have been blessed — usually by the older saints of the congregation — to hear feedback of joy and delight when I preach on giving. This is simply because these mature saints have *lived* the joy of generosity to the Lord's work and have seen the glorious fruit of this obedience in their own lives.

Misunderstandings about Giving

Misunderstandings about giving have been traditionally perpetuated in the local church. Probably the biggest of these comes from a lack of precise preaching and teaching about the covenants of Scripture. Jews, under the covenant that God made with Israel—later called the Old Covenant—were mandated to support the theocratic priestly government by giving ten percent of their produce twice per year and another ten percent every three years. This would mean an average of 23.33% of their income, labeled in the Old Testament as "the tithe," meaning "the tenth." In addition, separate free-will offerings were to be made as thanksgiving offerings and for other reasons.

But we don't live in a theocratic government, and we are no longer under the Old Covenant, but rather the New Covenant in Christ. To support the God-mandated governments under which we live, we are called not to pay a tithe but to pay taxes (Rom 13:1-7). Beyond this, we're called to generously support the work of preaching the gospel on earth. Jesus Himself was supported by the gifts of His followers. The apostles were also supported by the giving of the church. The first known dedicated church building was probably erected around AD 250 by the donations of local believers during a time of persecution. And 1 Timothy chapters 5 and 6 give vital information concerning how we are to generously, financially support the work of spreading and proclaiming the gospel of Christ.

I can easily make the case for giving as a New Covenant believer in Christ. But I *do* try to avoid the term "tithing" as it implies a mandated percentage and the continuation of the Old Covenant, neither of which is the case for New Covenant believers. Hebrews 8:13 says that, "in speaking of a new covenant . . . [God] makes the first one obsolete. And what is becoming obsolete and growing old is ready to vanish away." So, you can rest assured that for the remainder of this book, I will never suggest you *tithe*.

Worship and Giving

Giving and worship were inextricably linked in the eyes of the Old Testament saint. Just because Christians are not under the Law of Moses any longer certainly does not negate the principles of worship we see in action in the Old Testament. Because of the sacrificial system and the high value placed on the privilege of temple worship, an Old Testament Jew would not *dream* of coming to worship God without bringing a sacrifice or gift of some kind; to worship God *always cost something*. After all, God was sparing the life of a sinner, allowing the true believer to bask in the Lord's glory and forgiveness.

As Christians, our access to God has been granted by the sacrifice of Christ, but that does not mean worshiping God is *free*. The Old Testament saint didn't arrive as a guest in another person's home without bringing a gift—and he *certainly* didn't arrive at the house of the Lord without bringing a gift. But in Christ's church, many people decide not to sacrifice anything and yet still take advantage of the resources: fellowship, spiritual nourishment, Bible teaching by well-trained men, and a meeting facility for which others in the church pay. After a steak dinner at a fancy restaurant, you would never leave your bill at the table next to you for them to pay. Yet sadly, this is how many people treat the local church. Worship and giving really do go hand-in-hand.

Cynicism about Giving

A high degree of cynicism has been successfully sown into the fabric of Christ's church concerning giving. I'd like to suggest seven primary reasons for this worrisome suspicion and distrust.

1. *An assumption that the church or pastor is greedy.* Certainly, leaders are to guard against greed (1 Tim 3:3), but this does not mean that all mention of giving and money automatically reveals the sin of greed. This assumption is often characteristic of unbelievers who may attend church. Greed is not, however, defined as an abundance of money or resources; it is an attitude of *worshiping* that money. It is even possible to be dirt poor and still be greedy! Hebrews 13:5 says to "keep your life free from the *love* of money" (emphasis added). Giving to the church or the local church doing some sort of giving campaign for a ministry project does not inherently prove the heart-motive of greed. In fact, those who *withhold* their money from the church may in fact reveal a greedy heart.

2. *The belief that the local church should just "do without."* Some take a very frugal view of how the local church ought to function. However, this betrays the belief that the individual church member (with this attitude) is more important than kingdom work. Sometimes, new resources and materials should be deemed necessary to continue forward in the mission which God has given the church, and giving promotes the success of those goals. Why should our homes have porcelain tile bathrooms but the church facility cheap and unattractive features?

3. *Rightful offense at the prosperity gospel.* The prosperity gospel stands as one of the most heinous spiritual deceptions of our time. It is embodied by a way of thinking which says giving is meant to extravagantly line the pockets of those who are preaching. It hurts true Christians to witness a supposed minister of the gospel rake in millions of dollars per year in the name of telling people God wants to make them rich. It is offensive to see these false teachers misuse the Scriptures

concerning God's provision, causing us to even steer clear of those verses because of a negative association. And that hurt and offense can increase our cynicism toward giving to the local church body.

4. *Lack of understanding that giving is an act of worship.* It seems at times that the average American evangelical person most often thinks of worship as merely singing songs at church. Yet worship encompasses all of life and certainly all elements of a Christian worship service. This includes the element of giving, as already mentioned above.

5. *Fear that giving will prevent me from having enough resources for my family.* When money is tight, it can be very difficult to give to the church. I have said numbers of times to my own congregation, "At least give one dollar each month and plant one little seed (2 Corinthians 9) which the Lord can use for His glory." But the fact is, it may be embarrassing to receive an annual giving report that says you gave $12, so you might hesitate in fear and decide to not give anything.

6. *A low value placed on Bible preaching and evangelism.* In my own observation, the more mature a saint is, the more he has an urgency and responsibility to play a major role in seeing the Word of God proclaimed. He sees the worth of human souls, and he gives to be able to bring more souls to Christ. He understands that he will get what he pays for: giving little may result in shallow messages from a part-time pastor who's working a full-time job during the week. But giving much may bring the bountiful return of trained men who spend hours before the Lord to bring to His clear, penetrating, life-changing Word each week.

7. *A shallow understanding of the biblical gospel.* I have observed a simple trend: those in the church with a surface-level grasp of Scripture don't see the value in giving, while those whose roots sink deep into the doctrines of grace tend to be the most generous. They are saturated in how generous and gracious God has been with *them* in forgiveness of sin, and this urges them to return that kindness to the beloved Bride of Christ, the Church.

But I have one more reason for cynicism in the church toward giving—the real clincher for me. This reason is so pervasive and so important that I am beginning the series of reasons to give with this topic. I believe the top reason for suspicion toward giving is *the belief that I own anything, that my money is actually mine.* And this will take us into the meat of the book as we examine our first reason to give: Because of God's Ownership.

Chapter 2

Give Because of God's Ownership

The account of Jesus calling several of the disciples to follow Him, described in the book of Luke, concludes with a stunning finale. After demonstrating His power through miraculously enabling a large catch of fish, Jesus shifts His attention to Simon Peter, a partner with James and John in their prosperous fishing business. Jesus tells Peter, "Do not be afraid; from now on you will be catching men" (Luke 5:10). And here is the striking finale to that exchange: "And when they had brought their boats to land, they *left everything* and followed him" (v.11, emphasis added). Certainly the giving up of all earthly possessions wasn't a prerequisite for salvation, but there is the prerequisite of surrendering your *claim* on not only all earthly possessions, but also on anything which would keep you from following Christ wholeheartedly.

That is really the main focus of this book: the heart attitude of surrendering all things for the sake of Christ. And one of the most tangible ways we're called in Scripture to demonstrate this heart attitude is with the financial offerings we give to the Lord and to His work. Over the next few chapters, I'd like to examine *joyful generosity*—our response to God's grace. It is the duty of the believer in Christ to contribute financially to kingdom work, particularly to the front lines of that work, the local church.

I will be outlining reasons from Scripture that we are to give to the Lord, but you will notice that I will leave out a very simple reason: *because God commanded it.* This is arguably *the* best reason to give, but because of its straightforwardness, it would not provide you with an opportunity to really think through and digest the other reasons and how they apply to the whole of your Christian life.

Believers in Christ are *commanded* by God to give to His work. In 2 Corinthians 9:7, Paul writes, "Each one must give as he has decided in his heart, not reluctantly or under compulsion, for God loves a cheerful giver." The idea of "not reluctantly or under compulsion" is often misunderstood to mean pastors shouldn't preach on giving because they're trying to cause compulsion.

But this interpretation is incorrect. Rather than compulsion—which happens when someone wants you to give regardless of your attitude about it—pastors are called to motivate obedience from a right heart. Paul wasn't directing to only give if you want to; he was instructing the Corinthians to give with a *cheerful* heart as opposed to a reluctant heart. In other words, Paul was not saying, "If you have a reluctant heart, don't give." He was saying, "If you have a reluctant heart, repent and give from a *cheerful* heart."

To start thinking about the theology of giving, we must realign our view of what we *actually* own. To do that, we need a foundation of theology proper, the study of God, which will place giving into its correct perspective. Two factors concerning God which help us have correct perspective on giving are God's privilege and God's promise.

God's Privilege

What is God's privilege? What is the divine right of God? Before we determine the answers to these questions, we will let Psalm 24 provide a foundation for us. This Psalm neatly divides into three easily-understood sections: the all-holy God, the all-victorious God, and the all-possessing God.

The All-Holy God

Verses 3–6 begin with a question of worship. "Who shall ascend the hill of the LORD? And who shall stand in his holy place?" (v.3). This speaks of coming to the temple on the hill of the Lord and standing in the place where He meets His faithful. Who is able to do this? A sobering and difficult answer is provided. "He who has clean hands and a pure heart, who does not lift up his soul to what is false and does not swear deceitfully" (v.4). Clean hands speak of the righteousness of outward deeds, while a pure heart refers to an inner soul which is undefiled by sinful thoughts, wholly devoted to God. To "lift up his soul to what is false" is to have love or loyalty in one's heart for anything above the Lord. Swearing deceitfully speaks of a higher allegiance to a false god, to believe in the value of something above the value of the Lord. The person who does these things given in Psalm 24 is fit to worship God and receive His blessing.

But there is obviously a new problem that arises. If those are the requirements to be allowed the privilege of worship, then we are all doomed and cannot approach God! You do *not* have clean hands. You do *not* have a pure heart. You have *not* kept yourself from idolatry of the heart. Our only hope of being qualified and fit to be a worshiper of God is to have someone *else* stand in our place to qualify for us — and it is the Lord Jesus Christ who was made to be sin on our behalf so that "in him we might become the righteousness of God" (2 Cor 5:21).

Now, through Christ, a person *can* be a true worshiper without violating the pure holiness of God; those of genuine faith *can* enjoy open fellowship of the Lord. "Such is the generation of those who seek him, who seek the face of the God of Jacob" (v.6). The all-holy God both demands holiness of mankind and enables it in him.

The All-Victorious God

In verses 7-10, the reader is presented with a picture of a king entering his capital city after having won a great battle and gaining glory for himself.

> Lift up your heads, O gates! And be lifted up, O ancient doors, that the King of glory may come in. Who is this King of glory? The LORD, strong and mighty, the LORD, mighty in battle! Lift up your heads, O gates! And lift them up, O ancient doors, that the King of glory may come in. Who is this King of glory? The LORD of hosts, he is the King of glory!

The gates or doors of the city are personified as preparing themselves for the entrance of the King of glory. The King of glory is described as being mighty in battle; He has conquered all His enemies. And verse ten identifies this King of glory—it is God Himself!

To the Israelite reading David's psalm, this section would be reminiscent of the occasion King David brought the ark of the covenant, the symbol of God's presence among His people, back into Jerusalem after having achieved victory by God's power over Israel's enemies. We also see a Messianic flavor, though, because someday the King of glory—Jesus Christ—will have triumphantly defeated His enemies and will take hold of the earth with His throne in the capital city of Jerusalem once again.

We see that the all-holy God who demands holiness and the all-victorious God who demands submission to Himself is none other than the King of the earth. But why does God have the right to demand holiness and to demand to be King of the earth? Mankind and the earth were made perfectly, yet man rebelled against God and creation became tainted by sin. Thus, God's holiness has been violated. As part of this rebellion, God has allowed Satan to be, for a time, the prince of the power of the air (Eph 2:2), also called the ruler of this world (John 12:31). As Satan has led humanity to reject God in countless ways, so God is coming to take the earth back and to be the King of glory.

The All-Possessing God

"The earth is the LORD's and the fullness thereof, the world and those who dwell therein, for he has founded it upon the seas and established it upon the rivers" (Ps 24:1-2). "Fullness thereof" has the idea of "all that fills it." Anything and everything on the earth is the Lord's.

So, what is the privilege that God possesses? It is the fact that He owns *everything* and has total rights over *everything*. He has the right to graciously offer salvation, to cast people who reject Him into the eternal lake of fire, to rule what He has created, and to take back what belongs to Him. The implications of God's ownership are endless!

The point is this: Romans 6:16 says, "you are slaves of the one whom you obey." You are either a slave of sin or a slave of righteousness. You are either the slave of God or the slave of sin. God has loaned you clothes to wear, air to breathe, food to eat, water to drink, a place to live, a husband or wife, children, the intelligence and skill to earn money, and money itself. We *must* remove the notion from our minds and hearts that anything we have actually belongs to us; it does not. Everything we have been loaned is expected to be used to the glory of God. So the question is not, "How much of *my* money should I give to the church?" The real question becomes, "How much of *God's money* can I invest in His kingdom work?"

Matthew 6:19-20 says, "Do not lay up for yourselves treasures on earth, where moth and rust destroy and where thieves break in and steal, but lay up for yourselves treasures in heaven, where neither moth nor rust destroys and where thieves do not break in and steal. For where your treasure is, there your heart will be also." Regarding these verses John MacArthur comments, "Our treasures upon earth and our treasures in heaven can involve money and other material things. Possessions that are wisely, lovingly, willingly, and generously used for kingdom purposes can be a means of accumulating heavenly possession."[1]

God's privilege is that *He* owns everything and therefore has rights over it.

God's Promise

Psalm 50 contains one of the most well-known verses about God's ownership in our Bible, often quoted to give comfort when during a time of material need. "For every beast of the forest is mine, the cattle on a thousand hills" (v.10). This is true and does provide comfort when we're in need of God's provision, but it's not really the main point of the verse.

The first six verses of the psalm describe a heavenly courtroom scene in which God presides and renders judgment. In the first two verses, God summons His people of Israel to appear before Him. "The Mighty One, God the LORD, speaks and summons the earth from the rising of the sun to its setting. Out of Zion, the perfection of beauty, God shines forth" (vv.1-2). Next, there is a repeated summons and an affirmation of the right to judge that which God possesses. Court is brought to order:

> Our God comes; he does not keep silence; before him is a devouring fire, around him a mighty tempest. He calls to

the heavens above and to the earth, that he may judge his people: "Gather to me my faithful ones, who made a covenant with me by sacrifice!" The heavens declare his righteousness, for God himself is judge! (vv.3-6)

Once court is in session, God gives judgment, correction, and reproof, followed by His qualifications as both judge and witness against the sinful people. "Hear, O my people, and I will speak; O Israel, I will testify against you. I am God, your God. Not for your sacrifices do I rebuke you; your burnt offerings are continually before me" (vv.7-8). Israel is maintaining the sacrificial system and performing acts of worship such as observing the holy days and feasts and required sacrifices. However, they had been treating God as if He were one of the Canaanite pagan deities who needed a sacrifice of food and provision to sustain Him. In other words, there was a heart attitude of hypocrisy by acting as if God needed something from Israel and they were doing Him a favor. So, He reminds them that *He doesn't need anything from human beings.* Why? Because He already owns it all!

The people were behaving as though God was dependent on them, when in fact, the sacrificial system was meant to acknowledge that they were dependent on Him. Furthermore, God moves from a fairly mild correction to a serious indictment of those with fraudulent faith as He challenges their right to associate themselves with God's covenant people. He lists examples with the basic lesson being this: persons of true faith act in righteousness and purity.

To those who would ignore God's instruction (v.17), approve of wickedness (v.18), sin greatly with their tongues (v.19), gossip and slander (v.20), and harbor a low view of God (v.21), God gives a promise. Without repentance and a humble, contrite heart that heeds the true purpose of sacrifices for atonement, He vows a continual, eternal threat to them. "Mark this, then, you who forget God, lest I tear you apart, and there be none to deliver!" (v.22).

In stark contrast, God also utters a promise to those with genuine faith. "The one who offers thanksgiving as his sacrifice glorifies me; to one who orders his way rightly I will show the salvation of God!" (v.23). This is the true believer who is thankful for the mercy and grace of God's forgiveness. This is the one who instinctively wants to obey God out of love and "order his way rightly." This is the one to whom salvation is given, because his faith is genuine and his love for God is real.

We should not misunderstand the point of this psalm. God is *not* saying, "Stop giving your sacrifices to Me since I don't need them." Instead He says, "Offer your sacrifices with a true internal reality of thankfulness." Those who simply go through the motions of worshiping God without genuine faith in the Lord are incurring judgment on themselves, but those with saving faith ought to give with heart thankfulness and gratitude.

The Implications of God's Privilege and God's Promise

Being informed by God's *privilege*, that He owns everything, and God's *promise*, that He will judge false believers and reward true believers — *God* becomes bigger and *you* become smaller. When our view of Him is too small and our view of ourselves is too big, it reveals a lack of trust in His words of 2 Corinthians 9:8, "And God is able to make all grace abound to you, so that having all sufficiency in all things at all times, you may *abound in every good work*" (emphasis added).

But when God is big, infinite, the owner of all things, and is pleased with our gifts offered in humility and gratitude to Him, now we are in the magnificent place of dependence. Our hearts are able to cry out, "I have a gift I want to give to You because I'm so thankful for Christ and my salvation! I know You will make all grace abound to me!" The message of Psalm 50 says that God desires your hearts, a real internal reality of faith which is given only by the Holy Spirit in salvation. And we tangibly, joyfully show God our hearts with an internal gratitude *accompanied* by a sacrificial gift.

God's chief concern is His own glory, and toward that end, He will always finance His own glory. He will always provide for His name to be lifted up. And while He has apportioned to us some of His resources, He expects us to invest them wisely — to put to a worthy use all that He Himself already owns.

Chapter 3

Give Because of God's Grace

The concept of grace is one of the most important and theologically rich ideas in the Bible. While entire volumes have been written trying to plumb the depths of God's amazing grace, for our purposes, I will offer a simple definition: *The act of God giving salvation from sin to those who do not deserve it and cannot earn it.*

To see what God's Word says about grace and its relationship to heart attitudes toward money and giving, let's examine a familiar story in Matthew 19 about a rich young man who was a ruler. Many times this well-known passage is incorrectly interpreted to mean, "Be as generous as Jesus wanted the rich young ruler to be so that you, too, can have treasure in heaven." But that application misses the true reason for this episode in the ministry of Jesus. As any good story includes twists and turns, let's consider four surprises to the reader that reveal the real thrust of this story in the ministry of Christ.

The First Surprise

Jesus is headed toward Jerusalem for the last time, as He is about to die and be resurrected. Mark's gospel tells us Jesus is on the road to Jerusalem in the region of Peraea, east of the Jordan River, where He ministers to the people there. Unlike the parables Jesus had been communicating earlier, the record of events here is a real-life conversation, orchestrated by God as a key part of His teaching on salvation: "And behold, a man came up to him, saying, 'Teacher, what good deed must I do to have eternal life?'" (Matt 19:16).

Mark's gospel tells us that the young man comes *running* up to Jesus and kneels before Him. He shows an eagerness and enthusiasm to see Jesus, an initial show of humility. From the other gospel accounts we learn he is a ruler and very wealthy, but what kind of ruler was this man? Most likely, he was a leader in the religious life of a particular synagogue, perhaps not a scribe or Pharisee but simply an influential, wealthy citizen who had shown great fastidiousness concerning the Law of Moses. Because he was younger than the average synagogue ruler and had earned great wealth already, this would have made him a smashing success in the eyes of his fellow Jews. After all, he had achieved a religiously high position, great wealth in a relatively short period of time, and was a moral man with a sense of the importance of obeying the Law.

But something is missing. Though this man has achieved success religiously, socially, and financially, he still believes he has a lack. There is something not quite in place to secure his spot in the kingdom of God. So, he asks Jesus, "What good deed must I do to have eternal life?"

In perfect wisdom, Jesus immediately diverts the man's attention away from his own works and draws his mind to the divine standard of goodness by putting God in a completely different category. "And he said to him, 'Why do you ask me about what is good? There is only one who is good. If you would enter life, keep the commandments'" (v.17). Jesus asserts that *only God* can do what is good because *only God* is inherently good! He challenges the notion that this man could do anything to please God and instead begins to draw out the man's weakness. "Keep the commandments" says Jesus, not because this was how to earn salvation, but because even the young ruler recognized himself as a law-keeper who was still missing something. He takes the bait and replies with confidence, "Which ones?" (v.18).

In response, Jesus lists the sixth, seventh, eighth, ninth, and fifth commandments, as well as the mandate of Leviticus 19:18 to love one's neighbor as one's self. Why does He choose these commands in particular? Because they all focus on outward, observable behavior in relationship to other people. So, Jesus' answer stumped the man. In his mind, he had already mastered these requirements. It is obvious to the reader that this man had a self-righteousness problem, but Jesus is not just trying to point out self-righteousness; He is pointing the rich young ruler to the correct conclusion, that keeping the law will be *insufficient*.

The young ruler knows something is lacking. He knows he still does not qualify to enter the kingdom of God. He believes he has not yet attained a status of eternal life. Yet in his mind, he has kept the law. To this man, Jesus delivers the first surprise: *You have nothing God wants or needs – you are still lacking!*

Now, if anyone in Israel could have come close to pleasing the Lord and earning eternal life, it would have been this wealthy young man. He wasn't a liar, but rather self-deceived into genuinely believing he had kept the law. He was a religious leader in his community and no doubt also a financially-stable property owner. But his final question reveals the belief that he fell short: "What do I still lack?" (v.20). Jesus strips away all other possibilities. The man's wealth, position, and religiosity had done nothing for him, and he had *nothing* to offer God.

The Second Surprise

With all the young man's self-righteousness and thoughts of bringing something to God now taken away, Jesus puts His finger on the one thing preventing the man from entering the kingdom. He finds the undisclosed, hidden-away, secret sin of the one who thinks he always obeys the Lord, and He presents the man with two more commands. "Jesus said to him, 'If you would be perfect, go, sell what you possess and give to the poor, and you will have treasure in heaven; and come, follow me'" (v.21). The first command: sell all your possessions and give the money to the poor. The second command: break completely with your current lifestyle.

When Jesus told the man to "follow me," He didn't mean *metaphorically* worshiping Christ; He meant, "Come with Me. Walk down the road away from it all with Me." This would mean immediately abandoning his position in the synagogue, liquidating his entire fortune, selling his lands, and literally walking the path to Jerusalem with Jesus as He neared His death on the cross.

Someone might be thinking, "That's a ridiculous request! No one would ever do that!" Yet several chapters earlier, Matthew records a rich tax collector seated in his tax booth, surrounded by coins and cash, who was given the same instruction. What did he do? Matthew shares *his own* conversion story: "As Jesus passed on from there, he saw a man called Matthew sitting at the tax booth, and he said to him, 'Follow me.' And he rose and followed him" (9:9).

So, what would this rich young ruler do? "When the young man heard this he went away sorrowful, for he had great possessions" (19:22). He left grieved and distressed. Jesus had touched the one thing he refused to surrender. The request by Jesus does not mean poverty is godlier than wealth or that money is inherently evil or that some lavish act of benevolence will please God, but rather the second surprise statement: *God insists that you give up your idols.*

When Jesus asked the man about keeping the law's commands, He first addressed those which the man believed he could obey perfectly on the outside. However, Jesus then exposes the commandment which the man refused to keep, "You shall have no other gods before me" (Ex 20:3). This was the very first commandment listed by Moses, and the man not only failed to keep this command, but also failed to repent!

Earlier in Matthew, Jesus preached, "No one can serve two masters, for either he will hate the one and love the other, or he will be devoted to the one and despise the other. You cannot serve God and money" (6:24). This man had made a god of his wealth, and when faced with a choice he refused to forsake his god. Jesus revealed the true colors of the man's wicked heart while simultaneously providing the answer to eternal life. Not "be poor!" but "get rid of your other gods and repent of worshiping that which is not God!"

The question, "What must I do?" had been answered. All the man had to do was turn around, hand his servant the keys to his house, and follow Christ in faith. Getting rid of his money wasn't a way to earn salvation or achieve God's favor; it was merely proof that the true, living God was now the *only* God in his life. This man was one moment away from living forever in heaven, but he instead chose to burn in hell for all eternity. His pursuit of the god of money for a few more decades meant more to him than having treasure in heaven. God insisted he give up his idols, and he said no.

The Third Surprise

The prosperity gospel, so destructive and spiritually catastrophic, is widely successful in today's world because it plays into the human ego and human arrogance. This movement says that God wants His people to be healthy and wealthy, and that these are the *signs* that you belong to Him. It's really nothing new, but rather an effective deception fed by our natural selfishness.

So, when Jesus destroyed the spiritual logic common to New Testament Jews that wealth and prosperity were signs of God's approval, He astonished them. Certainly, they reasoned, the rich were the most likely to enter God's kingdom because of the earthly blessings they manifested. But this was not so. Matthew 19:23-24 continues the narrative, "And Jesus said to his disciples, 'Truly, I say to you, only with difficulty will a rich person enter the kingdom of heaven. Again I tell you, it is easier for a camel to go through the eye of a needle than for a rich person to enter the kingdom of God.'" It seems to be a unique temptation for the wealthy to continue worshiping their wealth. Based on the cultural belief that this rich, young ruler was the most likely candidate to please God, Jesus' disciples are flabbergasted! If this man wasn't worthy of salvation, then who would be (v.25)?

In verse 24, the idea of a rich person entering the kingdom of heaven is compared to a camel going through the eye of a needle. For centuries, pastors have amazed and astounded their congregations by presenting solutions to this impossible situation, but in so doing, they inadvertently proclaim a different gospel to their listeners. One interpretation proposes that the Greek word for camel is a misprint, being very similar to the word for "rope," so Jesus was saying a rich man entering heaven is like a rope being pulled through the eye of a needle. However, this is pure conjecture and there is no evidence for it.

Another idea for explaining this text is that the main gates of Jerusalem were kept shut and when travelers arrived they used a smaller gate, called the Needle Gate, to enter. To pass through the gate, a camel couldn't fit unless all its baggage was first removed. But there is no evidence of this type of gate on the outer walls of

Jerusalem, and even ones on the inside of the city that could be considered the "Needle Gate" were much too small for even a camel.

A third suggestion focuses on one's spiritual attitude — that like the camel getting on its knees to come through a city gate, a person had to humble himself and enter God's kingdom unencumbered. The problem is that this *still* places the lost, unsaved person as the one responsible for their salvation. What do all of these often-preached misinterpretations have in common? *That salvation is difficult but that it still humanly possible*; given enough time and effort, we could eventually unravel a rope and fit it through the eye of a needle, or force a small camel to bend down and stoop through a tiny gate. In other words, we could be saved if *we try really hard*.

The surprise answer Jesus gives to the question of who then could be saved is this: *No one! No one* can do anything to merit God's favor! *No one* can be saved! Jesus said, "With man, this is *impossible*" (v.26) because mankind is utterly incapable of reaching out to God. Why is salvation from sin impossible with mankind? I can offer four reasons.

We Were Spiritually Dead

When Adam lived in the Garden of Eden, God warned him not to eat of the tree of the knowledge of good and evil because immediate spiritual death would occur (Gen 2:16-17). Adam didn't physically die that day, but he was immediately subjected to the curse of God, bringing spiritual death to himself and all of mankind. Romans 5:12 states, "Therefore, just as sin came into the world through one man, and death through sin, and so death spread to all men because all sinned." Paul also graphically describes our spiritual deadness in Ephesians 2:1-3 when he writes, "And you were dead in [your] trespasses and sins...following the course of this world, following the prince of the power of the air...[you were] sons of disobedience...carrying out the desires of the body and the mind…by nature children of wrath." You did whatever your body and mind wanted because you were by nature a child of wrath headed for hell, just like the rest of the world.

King David confessed that he, too, was doomed from the start. "Behold, I was brought forth in iniquity, and in sin did my mother conceive me (Ps 51:5), and "The wicked are estranged from the womb; they go astray from birth, speaking lies" (Ps 58:3). Jesus addresses our spiritual deadness when He states we must be born again (John 3:7), and He uses a passive verb, meaning someone else has to do this *for* us. First Peter 1:3 affirms that the saved have been *caused* to be born again, which again proves we cannot reach out to God when we are spiritually dead.

We Had Polluted Minds and Infected Hearts

Consider the plethora of Scriptures concerning the real state of the minds and hearts of mankind:

- "The LORD saw that the wickedness of man was great in the earth, and that every intention of the thoughts of his heart was only evil continually" (Gen 6:5).
- "The intention of man's heart is evil from his youth" (8:21).
- "The hearts of the children of man are full of evil, and madness is in their hearts" (Eccl 9:3).
- "People loved the darkness rather than the light because their works were evil" (John 3:19).
- "For the mind that is set on the flesh is hostile to God, for it does not submit to God's law; indeed, it cannot. Those who are in the flesh cannot please God" (Rom 8:7-8).
- "Both their minds and their consciences are defiled" (Titus 1:15).
- "The natural person does not accept the things of the Spirit of God…he is not able to understand them" (1 Cor 2:14).
- "They are darkened in their understanding…due to their hardness of heart" (Eph 4:18).

We Were Enslaved to Sin and to Satan

John writes in John 8:44, "You are of your father the devil, and your will is to do your father's desires." Paul states in Ephesians 2:2, "in which [trespasses and sins] you once walked, following the course of this world, following the prince of the power of the air." He prays in 2 Timothy 2:26 that God would enable men to "escape from the snare of the devil, after being captured by him to do his will." John again writes in 1 John 5:19, "the whole world lies in the power of the evil one." Paul clarifies in Romans 6:20, "you were slaves of sin" and in Titus 3:3, "slaves to various passions and pleasures."

We Were Unable to Change Ourselves

Job laments that no one can turn something unclean into something clean (Job 14:4). Jeremiah says that just as a leopard cannot change its spots, so those accustomed to doing evil cannot suddenly do good (Jer 13:23). Jesus declares that a diseased tree has no ability to produce healthy fruit (Matt 7:18) and that no one can come to Christ unless the Father first draws him (John 6:44).

Thus, the Bible is crystal clear. We are incapable of reaching out to God because we were spiritually dead, we had a polluted mind and infected heart, we were enslaved to sin and to Satan, and we were unable to change ourselves. Who then can be saved? *With man, no one can! It is impossible!*

The Fourth Surprise

This leads us to the fourth and final surprise statement from Jesus: *with God all things are possible!* (v.26). God enables us to give up our *own* kingdom so that we can enter *God's* kingdom. Romans 8:14 says, "For all who are led by the Spirit of God are sons of God." Lydia, listening to Paul's preaching in Philippi, heard the message of the gospel and "the Lord opened her heart" (Acts 16:14). John writes in John 1:13 that believers are born again by the will of God. "He saved us, not because of works done by us in righteousness, but according to his own mercy, by the washing of regeneration and renewal of the Holy Spirit" (Titus 3:5). Peter says we have been born again (1 Pet 1:23), and John says we have been born of God (1 John 5:4). In 2 Corinthians 5:17, Paul tells believers "if anyone is in Christ, he is a new creation." "For as the Father raises the dead and gives them life, so also the Son gives life to whom he will" (John 5:21). And finally, Colossians 2:13 makes clear that "you, who were dead in your trespasses and the uncircumcision of your flesh, God made alive together with him, having forgiven us all our trespasses."

This is magnificent, incomparable, amazing grace! And this grace is lived out in the lives of those who *were* following Christ: "Then Peter said in reply, 'See, we have left everything and followed you. What then will we have?' Jesus said to them, 'Truly, I say to you, in the new world, when the Son of Man will sit on his glorious throne, you who have followed me will also sit on twelve thrones, judging the twelve tribes of Israel'" (Matt 19:27–28). Jesus assigns the apostles future leadership of the future-restored Israel, and then He makes a general announcement. "And everyone who has left houses or brothers or sisters or father or mother or children or lands, for my name's sake, will receive a hundredfold and will inherit eternal life. But many who are first will be last, and the last first" (19:29–30).

The rich, young ruler wanted to be first yet will end up last, facing this same Jesus in judgment when asked, "Why would you not stop worshiping your money?" He will be thrown into the lake of fire. But everyone who, by the grace and mercy of God, has repented of all they worship that is *not* God will be first, meaning they will have eternal life!

I said at the beginning of the chapter that this whole passage has one main point. In verse 21, Jesus said that the rich man had to give up his riches because they were an idol. In verse 24, He said that it was easier for a camel to pass through the eye of a needle than for a rich man to be saved. He said that with man, salvation is impossible. But here's the main idea — if you *are* a believer, then *you have threaded the needle!* You *have* given up all your idols to follow Christ, and God has plucked you out of your spiritual deadness and provided redemption for you! Consider this illustration from the Lord Jesus Himself:

> At that time the disciples came to Jesus, saying, "Who is the greatest in the kingdom of heaven?" And calling to him a child, he put him in the midst of them and said, "Truly, I say to you, unless you turn and become like children, you will never enter the kingdom of heaven. Whoever humbles himself like this child is the greatest in the kingdom of heaven. (Matt 18:1-4)

Does this mean we must be *innocent* like a child? No, because children are born with a sinful nature. However, a little child has nothing to offer and has eyes only for his parents. He has no idols, no power; he is utterly dependent on and will follow his parents wherever they go. God has made us like that little child and threaded the needle of the impossible. We cannot fully understand what being alive in Christ means unless we have first been dead in our trespasses and sins. In fact, this is such astounding news that 1 Peter 1:12 says it is something that even angels long to grasp.

The Connection of Grace to Giving

Now, what does this have to do with joyfully, generously giving to the local church? To answer that, let's consider briefly Luke 7, a time when Jesus was invited to dine at the home of a Pharisee. A woman of the city, a sinner who had sold her body and degraded herself in her depravity, found out that Jesus was going to be there and came, too. Likely the meal would have been held in an outdoor courtyard where spectators could attend and listen to the conversation, so she approached, sat, and listened. At the end of this event, Luke records that Jesus made the woman spiritually clean by forgiving all her sins. The reason she came to Jesus was because of her gratitude for Christ and for all that He had done in wiping her sins away, and what she did next showed her desperation to demonstrate this gratitude. She first wept over the feet of Jesus, kissing them in her thankfulness and humility, drying them with her own hair. Then she anointed His feet with expensive perfume. Her response to the grace of God was to give in extravagance because she understood what He had done for her.

We can't kiss the feet of Jesus. We can't anoint His feet with costly ointment. But we *can* give generously to the work of His kingdom in gratitude and thankfulness because of God's grace! Giving is grounded in the grace of God as an act of immense appreciation.

Chapter 4

Give Because of God's Provision

Think through this true story of a faithful local church. This Baptist church in the Midwest presents an example of persistence, gospel faithfulness, and a dogged determination to stay the course in their dedication to Christ and to one another. Constituted in 1903, the local body of believers began meeting in schoolhouses and local church buildings when other believers were not holding their own services. In 1918 one member donated some land, and the first church home was built.

However, in 1927 a tornado destroyed the building, and members assembled two months later to draw up plans for a new building while again meeting in other locations. About forty years later, the church decided to relocate to make room for expansion, and in the middle of construction in 1971, the new building was hit by another tornado. But the church continued to band together, and just eight years later they completed yet another new sanctuary. In 1983 and 1995, two multi-purpose buildings were added, and an updated sanctuary and children's facility were finished in 2006 and 2014, respectively.

Amid several church moves, two tornados, and multiple building projects, the church continued to move forward with gospel faithfulness. This type of story brings to light the need for giving — giving to the local church body in a real way as they sought to construct a building for meeting and gathering purposes. In looking at this church, as it facilitated capital campaigns for a new building, several observations could be made.

First, each time the church raised money together, it positively impacted the overall faithfulness and sanctification of the families. Second, they were able to create community attention and gospel opportunities. Third, they saw not only the building fund giving increase, but also the general giving fund and missions giving increased. And fourth, each time they walked through the process again, the congregation learned that many blessings from the Lord accompanied their effort, including eagerness to undertake a new project!

But as human beings, we have fears that can take us captive and prevent a church like this from moving forward in something like a building campaign. For example, there is the fear of the loss of fond and deeply rooted memories. There might also exist a fear that the personality of the church will change and the church identity will be lost. Both fears are alleviated, however, by going through the experience together. Old memories can still be cherished while new ones are created. And core values shouldn't change, since a church is supposed to be grounded in the Word of God rather than a location.

But there is another fear involved in giving to the needs and ministries of the local church — a very real and very personal fear: *that if I give, I might not have enough resources to meet my own personal needs*. We can categorize this as a fear of provision, and to counter it, we will explore the third reason to give, but before that, let's take a look at the challenges of a *wrong* view of God's provision.

The Prosperity Gospel Abuse of Scripture

The prosperity gospel movement has not helped with correctly understanding God's provision. Not only do prosperity gospel preachers and books deceive non-Christians with a false gospel by convincing people God exists to make them healthy and wealthy, but they also put a bad taste in the mouth of the saved. These charlatans abuse Scripture and push true believers away from particular passages and ideas as they twist what God's Word actually says.

For example, one master of abusing Scripture is Creflo Dollar, famous for hosting so-called worship services in which people approach him and throw money at him. In taking Bible verses completely out of context, he incorrectly interprets Scripture to mean what he wants it to mean and proclaims the idea that tithing (his term) equates with salvation. He has been documented saying there are people in his church who were unsaved, but they gave financially and "that tithe was so strong it hooked them to the blessing...You can't stay cursed [if you're] tithing...Every sinner I know who is tithing ends up saved." In another sermon, Dollar said he wished the church could legally line up all the non-tithers and have the tithers shoot them with machine guns, bury them outside, and then return to "have church and have the anointing."[2]

Creflo Dollar is among so many that preach a twisted view of giving, and they include in their message that God will give you great wealth if you give. We rightly are repelled by this disgusting mangling of the gospel message! Too many prosperity gospel heretics use the phrase "sow a seed" to mean "give to my ministry so that God can make you wealthy." The biblical text where that metaphor is originally found is thus taken out of its intended purpose, and many believers become *uncomfortable* with "sow a seed" because of the strong association with a false gospel. Yet all Scripture is inspired by God and useful for teaching, rebuking, correcting, and training in righteousness, so let's examine what this text *does* mean in its proper context.

> The point is this: whoever sows sparingly will also reap sparingly, and whoever sows bountifully will also reap bountifully. Each one must give as he has decided in his heart, not reluctantly or under compulsion, for God loves a cheerful giver. And God is able to make all grace abound to you, so that having all sufficiency in all things at all times, you may abound in every good work. (2 Cor 9:6–8)

In 1 Corinthians 16, Paul had appealed for financial help toward the Jerusalem relief fund. The city had been impoverished through the famines in Judea, and those in Corinth had promised to give but had not yet followed through. So, in 2 Corinthians 9, Paul writes them a reminder of their previous commitment. The members were ready, zealous, and inspirational to other churches even; the leaders had reminded them of their commitment and organized advance planning to receive their contribution. Now Paul presents specific guidance on the proper heart attitudes toward giving which give us confidence in the Lord's provision.

Heart Attitude 1: Give with Expectation

Paul outlines a simple proverb concerning the Lord's provision for His people and the relationship between provision and giving. "The point is this: whoever sows sparingly will also reap sparingly, and whoever sows bountifully will also reap bountifully" (9:6). He uses an agricultural metaphor to relate giving for the Lord's work with sowing or planting a seed. Before getting too far into the comparison, however, Paul speaks of sowing *sparingly*. This can be translated as "in a scanty or meager manner."[3] Other ideas of this particular word include "thriftily,"[4] "one who is stingy,"[5] or "frugally."[6] In other words, there is a *heart attitude* at stake here. This has nothing to do with dollar amounts or wealth, but rather with how you view giving to the Lord's work.

Even the English translation, "sparingly" is helpfully self-defining: "What can I *spare*? After I've taken care of everything else that is most important to me, what do I have *left*?" Paul is not necessarily automatically condemning this thinking, but he does make the point that if you sow sparingly, you will reap sparingly. If you have a heart attitude of being overly frugal in your giving, the Lord is not necessarily going to provide a lot more for you to give.

In the second half of the proverb, Paul says whoever sows bountifully will also reap bountifully. What does it mean to sow bountifully? This phrase is translated from three Greek words that mean "on the basis of blessing." One source defines it as "a large amount of something with the implication of blessing or benefit" and translates the verse to mean "the one who plants an abundance will reap an abundance."[7]

The most important feature here is the attitude of expectation—on the basis of blessing. Paul has in mind the blessing to sow bountifully with the hope of receiving a bountiful harvest and a return from the Lord. This is the same concept Paul gave in 1 Corinthians 9:10, which says concerning financial remuneration for ministers of the gospel, "Does he not certainly speak for our sake? It was written for our sake, because the plowman should plow in hope and the thresher thresh in hope of sharing in the crop."

But as later verses state, the reason for this bountiful harvest is not to promote personal enrichment, even though the Lord's provision may very well result in His personal blessing on you. Rather, the primary reason for the Lord's provision is allow the faithful to give more! The man who gives $25 and for whom this is a great and difficult sacrifice is sowing *bountifully*, while the man who gives $5,000 without feeling any discomfort whatsoever is perhaps sowing sparingly because Paul's primary concern is attitude, not amount.

A wise giver wants to maximize the effect of his gift and promote worthy and God-honoring causes. But we also must remember that our first and primary line of giving should be to the local church before giving to other organizations, even if those organizations seem to have a further-reaching or faster-return impact. God is the one who created the maximum effect, and our expectation of reaping a reward from the Lord will be honored when we give to His body, the church, the only "organization" that Christ promised to bless and make successful (Matt 16:18).

Heart Attitude 2: Give with Consideration

The second heart attitude Paul calls us to involves considering, giving with thoughtfulness and contemplation. "Each one must give as he has decided in his heart, not reluctantly or under compulsion, for God loves a cheerful giver" (2 Cor 9:7). We often understand "not reluctantly or under compulsion," but the previous phrase needs a closer look. In Greek, this text doesn't include a verb, so Paul would have been saying "when you give," not "if you give." In other words, the exclusion of the verb assumes that giving is happening in the life of "each one," *every* Christian.

Paul lays out three ways to give with consideration. He expresses one positively and two negatively. First, he explains how to give as a personal decision, "as he has decided in his heart." This verb form of "decided" in Greek stresses something done in and for one's own self, making a personal choice that is prayerfully believed to be the best course of action based on particular circumstances. There is great freedom which transcends the idea of a set percentage or amount, since each person knows his own heart, situation, and ability more than others understand. A decision of how much to give to the church is a personal decision before the Lord.

Second, Paul says to give "not reluctantly," which literally means not out of grief or sorrow. In other words, we aren't supposed to give away money which we need for rent or groceries, causing us to weep in anguish. If we shed tears along with our offering to the Lord, let them be tears of joy in the grateful worship of God!

Third, we are to give not "under compulsion." The translation here means out of force, distress, or duress. God is *not* wringing His hands over the fate of a church or threatening they must give "or else." While we are part of *Christ's* church and He holds us accountable for our faithfulness, we also know that the kingdom plan does not rest upon us, nor does God *need* us. Paul does not, however, forbid using strong appeals to give, since he is obviously making a direct petition here. Yet, he is calling the Corinthians to action by saying he would hate for them to embarrass themselves by stinginess. He wants them to give from a willing and eager heart.

What do you get when a believer gives with consideration, giving as a personal decision, not reluctantly, and not under compulsion? You get a Christian who is "a cheerful giver" (2 Cor 9:7). We derive the English word "hilarious" from this term, and though today we define "hilarious" as extremely funny or amusing, in even the recent past this word had much more to do with being merry and joyful. As well as the phrase, "You should give hilariously!" preaches, it is more accurate to see cheerful giving as giving which is joyful and happy. Giving is no longer just a mere budget item, giving now becomes a way to express your joy in Christ. So, if you are giving as a personal decision, not reluctantly, and not under compulsion, you are a cheerful giver, and the Lord loves this heart attitude!

Heart Attitude 3: Give with Anticipation

Paul continues in his heart attitude exhortation to the Corinthians: "And God is able to make all grace abound to you, so that having all sufficiency in all things at all times, you may abound in every good work" (v.8). One can't help but notice how many times Paul stresses completeness in this verse. "all grace...all sufficiency in all things at all times...every good work." This is best understood in the following logical statements:

- If you give with expectation and consideration, then you can expect God to make all grace abound to you and provide monetarily for you . . .
- And if God is providing monetarily for you, then you will have all sufficiency for everything you need . . .
- And if you have all sufficiency for everything you need, then you can abound, going over and above, in every good work.

Paul reminds us how God provides for His own by quoting Psalm 112:9, "As it is written, 'He has distributed freely, he has given to the poor; his righteousness endures forever'" (2 Cor 9:9).

What should we anticipate? Since the God who provides for your needs will also provide for what you *give*, we can anticipate the provision of God, perhaps even in an increasing manner. "He who supplies seed to the sower and bread for food will supply and multiply your seed for sowing and increase the harvest of your righteousness" (v.10).

Randy Alcorn tells the story of a small business owner who made about $50,000 in annual profit. After attending a conference and being challenged to give $1,000,000 to the cause of seeing people won to Christ, he and his wife decided to set a goal of giving the equivalent of their annual profit the next year. Eleven months passed by and the couple still wasn't close to reaching this goal, until they received a surprise on the *last day of December*, enabling them to make the $50,000 goal. The Lord continued to provide and they continued to give away proportionate to what God gave them, and within a few years, they passed the $1,000,000 mark in their giving.[8]

God was not providing for this couple's needs so that they could live an opulent, affluent life. He was providing for them so that they could be funnels of God's resources for the gospel! In joy, they reached the point where they were giving away many times more than what they had kept, born simply out of a desire to give to the work of spreading the biblical gospel. Not one believer will arrive in heaven and be reprimanded by God for giving too much to the work of the kingdom!

Some of the benefits of giving are presented in Paul's few verses:

> You will be enriched in every way to be generous in every way, which through us will produce thanksgiving to God. For the ministry of this service is not only supplying the needs of the saints but is also overflowing in many thanksgivings to God. By their approval of this service, they will glorify God because of your submission that comes from your confession of the gospel of Christ, and the generosity of your contribution for them and for all others. (2 Cor 9:11–13)

Your giving will create material and spiritual blessing; your needs will be met; you will be a blessing to the church. All this together produces worship, which properly points the focus heavenward to the glory of God for His mercy and kindness. Verses 14–15 state, "While they long for you and pray for you, because of the surpassing grace of God upon you. Thanks be to God for his inexpressible gift!" This is extremely important because Paul ends climatically by making a connection between the material provision of God and the greater gift: the gift of *Jesus Christ His Son*.

In Christ, you are justified and considered righteous and pure. You have received forgiveness of all your sins; you are called to His eternal glory. You are sanctified and set apart for God's purposes; you have been given the Holy Spirit who remade your heart and has sealed you for heaven. You have received an eternal inheritance; you possess a spiritual forever-family in the church;

you are put into the legal will of God as a co-heir with His Son over a glorious kingdom. You are perfectly safe at the moment of your death and will be instantly in His presence; you will reign with Him in the future kingdom after His return. You will not be judged at the final Great White Throne judgment of Revelation 20; you will be kept far from the eternal lake of fire prepared for the devil and his angels and all who have rejected Christ. You will walk on New Earth and look up at New Heaven; you will walk the streets of New Jerusalem and reign forever alongside Christ.

Now *that* is an inexpressible and indescribable gift! It is actually quite easy for Paul to say, "When you give generously, the Lord is going to provide for you and multiply your gift—look at the indescribable gift of salvation He's already given you!"

Showing a True Belief in God's Provision

Hopefully, I have made the case that God *will* provide for you, particularly as you faithfully give to him with the heart attitudes I outlined. But how can you demonstrate you really believe this? Your church, whether it is the general fund which provides for your pastors and other ministry needs, or a special project such as a building campaign or missions project, can benefit from your true belief that God will provide. Let me challenge you to make a simple record of God's provision as related to your faithfulness to give. This record would consist simply of two columns: what you give and how the Lord provides. You can include the dates for each time you give and each time the Lord provides something extra for you to give. I challenge you to stay faithful to this for three years. Then look and see if the Lord did not do all He said He would do in 2 Corinthians 9!

If fear is keeping you from giving, lay aside those fears and trust the Lord for your provision. He will *not* fail you!

Chapter 5

Give Because of God's Church

God made every pastor differently. All pastors who are attempting to following God's will for the gospel ministry should share some common qualities, but there are particular emphases and loves which each pastor holds unique and which motivates him. Personally, other than love for the Lord and a desire to please Him, one of the biggest motivators for me as a pastor is the idea of happy church members. By my simple definition, happy church members are those who are conforming their lives to the Lord in Christlikeness. They are humble, eager to learn and grow, and function as joyful and pleasant partners in the gospel ministry. It's no coincidence that the characteristics of healthy, joyful church members are the same criteria found in Scripture. One of these qualities, my focus in this chapter, is that they give honor to their leaders. Let's examine the church's gift *from* God, the church's gift *to* God, and the church's faith *in* God.

The Church's Gift from God

In Ephesians 4, the Apostle Paul tells us some of the effects of Christ's ascension to heaven. "Therefore it says, 'When he ascended on high he led a host of captives, and he gave gifts to men'" (Eph 4:8). The host of captives speaks of all who would subsequently follow Christ by faith. Some people believe "and he gave gifts to men" refers to spiritual gifts, such as the speaking and serving gifts listed in Romans 12. But the immediate context makes it clear that these gifts to the church are really *men*. "And he gave the apostles, the prophets, the evangelists, the shepherds and teachers" (v.11).

We don't need the apostles and prophets anymore because we have a completed Bible, called "the apostles' teaching" in Acts 2, and evangelists speaks primarily of church-planting men who proclaim the gospel to peoples who haven't yet heard of Christ. The shepherds, or pastors, and teachers are then left to do the wonderful work of teaching and maturing the people of God. There is some debate over whether the term "pastor-teachers" is a better interpretation of the Greek grammatical construction, but suffice it to say that while there may be teachers in the church who are not pastors, there should never be a pastor who is not a teacher.

As a side note, the shepherds of the church are to be men, made clear in the qualifications of elders in 1 Timothy 3 and Titus 1. Also, the pastors and shepherds, the overseers, and the elders are all terms used interchangeably in the New Testament. There is no hierarchy of one type of shepherd being in authority over other types of shepherds; the elders are equal in authority, forming a leadership team. So why should we view church shepherds as a gift from God to Christ's church? Let me outline several reasons.

The Bible Says So

Ephesians says they are a gift from God. Verse 11 tells us Christ "gave" these men, meaning He granted the church something. It was a divine favor, a blessing, a delight to the church. There really is not much more to say about this; Scripture lacks no clarity on the matter. The shepherds of the church stand as the gift Christ gave to us to teach and mature us in the ways of the Lord. In my own congregation, I have been so blessed to observe an uncanny phenomenon: the members who are fed and nourished with the Word of God develop a quite inexplicable affection for me and others who teach them. Through experience, they have discovered that the shepherds of the church are truly a gift from Christ.

For Their Calling

The question is sometimes asked, "Who chooses the pastors of the church?" Quite simply, *God does*. I believe wholeheartedly in the idea of a call to gospel ministry, and Scripture certainly bears this out. For example, all of the apostles were designated and called by Christ. Some men have a call to full-time vocational ministry and others to the important task of leadership while financially self-supporting themselves. First Timothy 3:1 says, "The saying is trustworthy: If anyone aspires to the office of overseer, he desires a noble task." Where does this desire come from, this yearning in the hearts of men in which they cannot do anything else? It comes from God, and it is accompanied by gifting to fulfill that call. Dr. John MacArthur tells of his calling in this way.

> I'm afraid not to be a pastor. And that's the truth. When I was 18, God threw me out of a car going 70 miles an hour. I landed on my backside and slid 110 yards on the pavement. By the grace of God, I wasn't killed, and by the grace of God, I was committed to become a pastor, because prior to that I knew the Lord had called me to that. I was being rebellious, and I decided if the Lord is going to fight like that, I'm going to give in and be a pastor, or whatever else He wants me to be. Every time I scratch my back I feel the scars of that, because they're still there to remind me that I should be

faithful to the pastorate, or there might be another highway somewhere in my future.[9]

For Their Training

We don't insist that leaders in the church all have seminary educations; some are self-taught while some are well-discipled in the context of the church. But for many centuries, the Lord has been training men in a seminary context to greatly accelerate their learning and growth for the purpose of shepherding God's people. Paul recalls that Timothy had to be "trained in the words of the faith and of the good doctrine that you have followed" (1 Tim 4:6). For the most part, well-trained men are not standing in pulpits making up information; they are studying and explaining the intricacies and nuances of Scripture. They are men who devote themselves to being saturated in the Bible so that they can take 20 or more hours of study and explain it to their congregations in 45–50 minutes. This takes tremendous skill and effort developed and honed over many years.

For Their Testing

Second Timothy 2:15 says, "Do your best to present yourself to God as one approved, a worker who has no need to be ashamed, rightly handling the word of truth." Being approved has the idea of having been preceded by testing. A man doesn't decide one day, "I think I'll be a leader in the church." He is to be trained, tested, and approved. This testing can and should take many forms. There is the testing of life itself, of how a man responds to the challenges and trials of life. There is the testing of patience and humility, of how a man has responded to opportunities to be a humble servant in the church rather than in charge of anything. And there is the testing provided by qualified leaders. In seminary, none of my professors simply lectured and said, "Well, I hope you got a lot out of this class." Rather, they made us write papers and take tests to *demonstrate* that we had in fact gotten a lot out of the class. In the local church, qualified leaders should test potential leaders as well. And a man coming through this testing successfully should be appreciated by the local church membership.

For Their Burden

In multiple places in the New Testament, pastors and elders are given the duty of leading and shepherding. Scripture doesn't merely give gentle life-advice for them—they must lead spiritually by their example in both vision and labor. "Obey your leaders and submit to them, *for they are keeping watch over your souls, as those who will have to give an account*" (Heb 13:17a, emphasis added). In 2 Corinthians, Paul describes the great anxiety he had for the churches under his care and the weightiness of seeing sin, pride, rebellion, fear, and slowness to learn in the body of Christ. He begs God for the continued sanctification of the members. A pastor should have friends within his church, but he is always a shepherd *first*. This is why Hebrews continues, "Let them do this with *joy* and not with groaning, for that would be of no advantage to you" (v.17b, emphasis added).

MacArthur sheds light by reflecting on Hebrew 13:17.

> That's a very strong statement, and a very formidable one for a person in spiritual leadership…We have a sobering duty. We will give an account before God. That's a tough enough thing to have to live with…I am accountable to God for the condition of the sheep. I am accountable to God for the decisions that I make. And we as a group [of elders] are accountable to God for what we decide, as we seek the wisdom of the Spirit…So he says, "Obey." Stubborn, self-willed people will steal the joy of their pastors, and give them grief…You want a miserable church? Have a miserable pastor. You want a miserable pastor? Don't submit, and you'll take his joy away, and he'll be a miserable man, and you'll be a miserable people.[10]

For Their Life-Changing Ministry

Paul describes the process of being changed into the image of Christ in 2 Corinthians 3:18: "And we all, with unveiled face, beholding the glory of the Lord, are being transformed into the same image from one degree of glory to another. For this comes from the Lord who is the Spirit." And how does this transformation happen? How are we beholding the glory of the Lord? This happens in and through the Word of God which is preached, taught, repeated, and exalted. In fact, the Light of the world is also called the Word of God in the flesh. God has raised up men to teach us of the glories of Christ, and this changes us to *be like Him*.

In summary, we view the church's shepherds as God's gift because the Bible says so, for their calling, for their training, for their testing, for their burden, and for their life-changing ministry. Here's the point: this flies in the face of the modern idea that pastors are merely employees of the church. They do not work for the church; they work for the Lord at the pleasure of the local church and for the benefit of the local church.

What should happen as a result of these gifts of men to the church? The next few verses in Ephesians 4 give us a quick survey. God activates the church, He unifies the church, He protects the church, He sanctifies the church, and He grows the church:

> To equip the saints for the work of ministry, for building up the body of Christ, until we all attain to the unity of the faith and of the knowledge of the Son of God, to mature manhood, to the measure of the stature of the fullness of Christ, so that we may no longer be children, tossed to and fro by the waves and carried about by every wind of doctrine, by human cunning, by craftiness in deceitful schemes. Rather, speaking the truth in love, we are to grow up in every way into him who is the head, into Christ, from whom the whole body, joined and held together by every joint with which it is equipped, when each part is working

properly, makes the body grow so that it builds itself up in love. (Eph 4:12-16)

Verse 12 explains that the ministry is the job of members while the minister's job is to equip them by means of the preached Word. Paul explains in verse 13 that unity is based in sound doctrine, which has Christ at its core. In verse 15, we become truth-bearers to the world and to one another, providing accountability and positive examples for each other. And as verse 12 already covered *spiritual* growth, verse 16 covers *numerical* growth.

All of this is rooted in the fact that Christ gave gifts to men. None of those blessings happen without the preached *Word* of God from *men* of God who have been given the spiritual *gifting* of God, and the result is a healthy *church* of God. No wonder Satan has gone after the pulpits of the world by diluting them with imposters and mocking them in movies and television. There is literally no more important job on earth than the faithful proclamation of the Word of God upon which the functioning of the church depends!

The Church's Gift to God

Now that we've examined the church's gift *from* God, let's turn to the church's gift *to* God. First Thessalonians 5:12-13 records the words of Paul, "We ask you, brothers, to respect those who labor among you and are over you in the Lord and admonish you, and to esteem them very highly in love because of their work. Be at peace among yourselves." In these verses, Paul instructs the church that they have three duties toward the leadership of the church. First, they are to respect them, which indicates knowing and understanding their hearts. Second, they are to esteem them, meaning regarding them in love. Third, they are to be at peace among themselves, which allows the leaders to focus on the work of the ministry rather than constantly breaking up squabbles.

Paul writes additional instructions and details in 1 Timothy 5:17-18, "Let the elders who rule well be considered worthy of double honor, especially those who labor in preaching and teaching. For the Scripture says, 'You shall not muzzle an ox when it treads out the grain,' and, 'The laborer deserves his wages.'" Here is a description of the elders in the church. "Honor" in this context speaks not only of respect and high regard but of money. Several other times in the New Testament, this Greek word is also associated with money (e.g., Matt 27:6, 9 and 1 Cor 6:20), and the context here of verse 18 makes it obvious Paul is discussing wages.

So why doesn't Paul use the term "money"? Why does he choose to use the term "honor" instead? To begin with, he is driving at heart motivation. We can't give money *without* giving honor, and this phrase encompasses both. Also, if Paul only spoke directly about money, it might come across as insensitive. Some of the other ways Paul refers to money include "fellowship" (Corinthians, Galatians, Philippians), "generous gift" (2 Cor 8:20), "sow, reap, grace" (2 Cor 8-9), "gift/blessing" (9:5), "good work" (9:8), "seed" (9:10), "harvest of righteousness" (9:10), "good things" (Gal 6:6), and "gift" (Phil 4:17). Here he calls it *honor*, conveying a sense of love, intimacy, and spiritual significance.

Does this mean a church should pay all its elders? Not necessarily, but for the teaching pastor, it would be extremely difficult and ineffective to *not* pay him, and he has the right to receive honor if he so chooses. In 1 Corinthians 9:11-12, Paul defends his ministry and the freedom he has to receive financial remuneration. He spends twelve verses defending his right to be paid, arguing that if you receive food and pay for it, and if you receive a place to live and pay for it, don't those who give you spiritual food have even *more* claim to be paid because they are imparting eternal things?

But because the Corinthians were critical of Paul's ministry, he didn't want to give them any other reasons to be harsh with him and thus he continues, "Nevertheless, we have not made use of this right, but we endure anything rather than put an obstacle in the way of the gospel of Christ" (1 Cor 9:12). An elder can choose to be self-supporting if he wishes.

We also see that there seems to be a difference, not in authority or importance but in function, between the general category of pastor or elder and the unique category of those who work extra hard at preaching and teaching. These men are said to be worthy of "double honor" (1 Tim 5:17). This doesn't mean giving vast wealth, private jets or world cruises to the pastor, but neither does this mean *undervaluing* the preached Word of God by categorizing his role alongside that of other professions. The ministry is *not* a profession; it *cannot* be compared to anything else because the impact of the pastoral ministry is quite literally *eternal*. It is the faithful preaching of the gospel which acts as the catalyst for salvation in Christ through the Holy Spirit and for the sanctification and Christlikeness of believers. That is value that cannot be measured in human terms.

The value of the ministry surpasses the value of other things because of the spiritual nature. The government might label what pastors are paid as a "salary," but that is not the idea conveyed in Scripture. Paul says that "the laborer deserves his wages" (5:18) to make the point that if we value the ox treading out grain, how much *more* should the shepherding of God's people be valued? Furthermore, *pastoral ministry is not an exchange of money for services provided*. That would be impossible to quantify. For example, if a pastor spends extra hours in prayer one week, should he be paid more? Or for example, if a particular text of Scripture I preach is one I am familiar with already, should I be paid *less* than if I preach a text which took many more hours of diligent study to prepare? Obviously, it is impossible to meaningfully quantify an exchange of money for services rendered.

Double honor speaks of "honor upon honor." This is due to the men who have been called by God into the role of leading, preaching, and teaching while giving up other pursuits. They give up these other pursuits so they can minister to the church completely unhindered, often undertaking other extended ministry God provides. For this they are to receive "honor upon honor." This double honor exists to free the man of God to be as impactful and render as much influence as possible. This is the picture of a *man* called by God, honoring Him by pouring his life into the preaching and teaching of Scripture and of the *people* of God, honoring Him by pouring their resources into the preaching and teaching of Scripture. The preaching is as unto the Lord, and the giving is unto the Lord!

Once again turning to the seasoned wisdom of MacArthur, he characterizes honor as being a gift of thanks back to the Lord:

> I know you pray for me. I know you care for me. I know that. I owe a debt of gratitude to God for that, because I'm not worthy of that, but I understand that. That goes with the territory of being a channel through which the grace of God can flow to people. Though it is God doing it all, and God's Spirit doing it all, as the thanks is passed back to God, somehow it gets passed through the channel that it came through. That's a wonderful and exhilarating reality.[11]

Many people have attempted to quantify what a pastor should or should not be paid for based on formulas or career comparisons. Some compare pastors to schoolteachers and others to administrators or executives. Endless views abound in this regard, but the problem is that these ideas are based on an arbitrary standard which is based on pure opinion. Scripture says to give honor and make it honor upon honor; therefore, armed with a godly attitude and a proper valuation of the gospel ministry, elders make their best judgment. And for the church member who has cultivated an attitude of giving which shows appreciation and double honor, there is never a sense of bitterness or resentment but rather one of continual joy. They have the attitude MacArthur describes:

> You esteem your elders, your pastors, and your esteem for them has no limits. Whatever level of appreciation you have now, increase it in love. You are to love them because of what they do. And if you do not, you're in disobedience to these direct words of Scripture. That love means you seek their best. That love means you overlook their weaknesses and frailties. That love means you speak well of them. That love means you encourage them. That love means you lift them up as called men of God, who have brought to you the truth.[12]

The Church's Faith in God

Having examined the church's gift *from* God and the church's gift *to* God, let's pull it all together to think on the church's faith *in* God. The book of Philippians can be rightly characterized as a thank-you note from Paul to the church of Philippi for its generous financial support of his ministry. The church at Philippi had the faith to believe they could be effective in gospel proclamation. And since the founding of the church in Acts 2, this faith has been expressed in a partnership between the shepherds of God and the sheep of God.

Paul shares his gratitude to the Lord for these believers. "I thank my God in all my remembrance of you, always in every prayer of mine for you all making my prayer with joy, because of your partnership in the gospel from the first day until now" (Phil 1:3-5). In verse 5, partnership primarily means financial remuneration, and Paul uses the same root word later when he writes, "you are all *partakers with me* of grace" (v.7, emphasis added). What are the Philippians supporting? Verse 7 continues and gives the answer: Paul's imprisonment and the defense and confirmation of the gospel.

In chapter 4, Paul says that the church at Philippi was the only church that was supporting him (4:15) and that "I have received full payment, and more. I am well supplied" (v.18). Was the church supporting Paul because he was a great person? No, they were partnering with him in the proclamation of the gospel of Christ, which produced joy for everyone! MacArthur states eloquently, "Whatever the church is of beauty, whatever the church is of joy, whatever the church is of effectiveness, whatever the church is of power is dependent initially upon the relationship between the shepherds and the sheep, the sheep and the shepherds."[13]

But before I close out this chapter, I want to add a final thought which I pray will penetrate your heart concerning the souls of the lost in your community.

Giving Specifically to a Building Campaign: An Evangelistic Reason

I'd like to look a little more specifically at giving to the local church in regards to a building campaign. In such a large undertaking, there is a high-level, heavenly reason for giving that has to do with the wonderful partnership between the shepherds and the sheep. One of the outcomes of the gift of men by God is that the church grows numerically through membership. Someone might argue, "We shouldn't aim for numerical growth," and I would agree that this shouldn't be the goal in and of itself. That is a pride-centered goal. But we *should* aim for the growth of the church through new believers who hear the gospel of Christ through this ministry!

If the statement "We shouldn't aim for numerical growth" is taken to its logical conclusion, then we should just lock the doors and tell everyone outside *we are content with them going to hell*! We should just keep the gospel as *our* treasure and keep it hidden where *we* are comfortable. But this is a grotesque twisting of what the gospel truly means! Giving to a new or improved building facility demonstrates the understanding that the lost are dying without

Christ and the church is the means by which God gathers in the elect! Jesus told the disciples that they would be fishers of men, and to illustrate what he meant Jesus told them to cast their nets into the water.

> And when they had done this, they enclosed a large number of fish, and their nets were breaking. They signaled to their partners in the other boat to come and help them. And they came and filled both the boats, so that they began to sink. But when Simon Peter saw it, he fell down at Jesus' knees, saying, "Depart from me, for I am a sinful man, O Lord." For he and all who were with him were astonished at the catch of fish that they had taken. (Luke 5:6-9)

If the Lord gives the opportunity to give to the local church, the prayers of the believers should be to *see* the pulpit on fire with the exaltation of the King of kings and the Lord of lords—to *hear* the life-giving words of the offer of eternal life—to *feel* the love of the body of Christ in our singing and fellowship—to *smell* the sweet fragrance of the gospel—and to *taste* and see that the Lord is good.

Chapter 6

Give Because of God's Reward

The goal of this book has been to build a robust theology of giving. We don't want to shrink away from this topic as if it is the one area of Christian growth and maturity which is nobody else's business. The scope of your *entire* life is the Lord's business, since everything in life is addressed in Scripture. The reason for building this theology together is to inform our hearts. For some it's simply a welcomed spiritual reminder. For others, it may be a call to change your hearts concerning giving when you are presented with a specific opportunity. To a believer, giving is a joy because of the understanding we have of what Christ has done for us.

One of the most insidious things about false doctrine is that it takes truths from Scripture and slightly massages them into error. This has the effect of sometimes causing believers to shy away from actual truth. When we hear a preacher say, "Let's put some treasure in heaven!" we shrink back and want to recite the doctrines of grace which is our safe place. But where did the idea of treasure in heaven originate? It came from the mouth of Jesus our Lord, and it wasn't just a concept or discussion. The idea of laying up treasure in heaven is a *command* of the Lord to His people as given in Matthew chapter 6.

Jesus preaches the Sermon on the Mount as recorded in Matthew 5-7, much of which describes characteristics of kingdom citizens. He emphasizes that the kingdom has not yet come to earth, meaning our total mind and heart and investment shouldn't be set on earthly things but on the heavenly things to come. Today, we speak of being heavenly-minded, that is, setting our hearts and affections on Christ's future kingdom and on our immediate future in heaven after our death. We have numerous reminders in the New Testament of this heavenly-mindedness:

- "If then you have been raised with Christ, seek the things that are above, where Christ is, seated at the right hand of God. Set your minds on things that are above, not on things that are on earth. For you have died, and your life is hidden with Christ in God. When Christ who is your life appears, then you also will appear with him in glory" (Col 3:1-4).
- "But our citizenship is in heaven, and from it we await a Savior, the Lord Jesus Christ" (Phil 3:20).
- "But as it is, [Old Testament saints] desire a better country, that is, a heavenly one. Therefore God is not ashamed to be called their God, for he has prepared for them a city" (Heb 11:16).
- "I press on toward the goal for the prize of the upward call of God in Christ Jesus" (Phil 3:14).

Where our minds and hearts reside tells us the state of our souls. Jesus gives a simple test in this regard: *where is your treasure?* What is most important to your heart? Is your treasure on earth or in heaven?

Is Your Treasure on Earth?

Set in the middle of the Sermon on the Mount, Jesus commanded, "Do not lay up for yourselves treasures on earth, where moth and rust destroy and where thieves break in and steal" (Matt 6:19). Jesus uses that which is *tangible*, our "treasure" or financial resources, to measure the *intangible*, our hearts. He first gives a negative injunction and defines treasure on earth in terms of its temporal and unprotected nature. "Where moth" can destroy speaks of the wealth of fine clothing, which in the Ancient Near East was basically a form of currency. "Where rust" can destroy comes from a Greek word that means consuming, related to the idea of something being eaten. Rust can also be translated as a "worm," which is a creature that would consume the object. Some even think it can refer to rodents eating stored grain. Whether it means the corrosion which attacks metallic objects or rodents invading granaries, storehouses, and harvest goods, the idea of being consumed is clear. "Where thieves break in and steal" brings the idea that if bugs and rodents haven't found a person's wealth, robbers and thieves might.

Jesus' point is clear: material possessions may appear substantial and lasting, but they are subject to loss in a number of ways. We are not to set our hearts on these things but rather to hold them loosely. What did Jesus mean by the prohibition "Do not lay up for yourselves treasures on earth"? He is *not* saying we should go about daily work without care and diligence or that business owners shouldn't try to make a profit or that we shouldn't reasonably save for the future. He is *not* saying we should feel guilty about enjoying good things on earth, which would go against the 1 Timothy 6:17 statement of God richly providing everything for us to enjoy. But He *is* saying that to hoard and enjoy all things only for ourselves is sinful, and it reveals the true state of our hearts.

Where do you draw the line? When do possessions become treasure on earth? When our hearts are consumed with these things to the neglect of greater, more eternal things. Proverbs 23:4 says, "Do not toil to acquire wealth; be discerning enough to desist." One of the ways God taught this lesson to Israel was through the Sabbath law, a day in which the people were not supposed to go about the business of earning money but to trust the Lord instead. The New Testament has a parallel lesson in Hebrews 13:5, "Keep your life free from love of money, and be content with what you have, for he has said, 'I will never leave you nor forsake you.'"

The wealthiest believer in the world and poorest believer in the world have something in common: "Naked I came from my mother's womb, and naked shall I return. The LORD gave, and the LORD has taken away; blessed be the name of the LORD" (Job 1:21). The rich may be tempted to look down on the poor with contempt and disdain, and the poor may be tempted to look down on the rich with envy and jealousy, but we *all* cross the finish line of life exactly penniless. Of course some people might leave more wealth behind for their children and families, but they, too, will die penniless.

If Jesus had only commanded, "Do not lay up treasures on earth," He would be giving the impression that material possessions in and of themselves are wicked, and it's obvious that is not what He's communicating. He is talking about how our use of material possessions reflects what is important to us. So He provides a second, positive step.

Is Your Treasure in Heaven?

Jesus continues, "But lay up for yourselves treasures in heaven, where neither moth nor rust destroys and where thieves do not break in and steal" (Matt 6:20). There is absolutely no danger to this kind of treasure. No moth, no rust, no thief can get to it—it is impervious to outside risk. The location of our treasure indicates the location of our hearts, the seat of our loyalties, the real home we cherish. Three key sub-questions fall under the heart-test question of heavenly treasure.

What is Our Treasure in Heaven?

Certainly our greatest treasure is Christ Himself who is all-satisfying and all-consuming, but in His mercy, God is building heavenly wealth for believers as well. Generally speaking, heavenly reward is often pictured in the New Testament as a crown—a symbol of royalty and right, in line with God's plan for mankind to be the vice-regents of the earth. The specific word for crown, or wreath, speaks of a crown presented to athletes, specifically runners, after they had finished a race victoriously. In the Bible there seems to be categories of crowns as well.

First, we could consider *the crown imperishable* as described in 1 Corinthians 9:25-27. "Every athlete exercises self-control in all things. They do it to receive a perishable wreath, but we an imperishable. So I do not run aimlessly; I do not box as one beating the air. But I discipline my body and keep it under control, lest after preaching to others I myself should be disqualified." The New Testament also speaks of the *crown of boasting*, given in 1 Thessalonians 2:19. "For what is our hope or joy or crown of boasting before our Lord Jesus at his coming? Is it not you?" This seems to be speaking specifically of the work of evangelism for those who have faithfully proclaimed the gospel of Christ.

Then we should remember the *crown of longing*. Second Timothy 4:8 says, "Henceforth there is laid up for me the crown of righteousness, which the Lord, the righteous judge, will award to me on that day, and not only to me but also to all who have loved his appearing." This crown seems to be for those who have been heavenly-minded and lived like it. Some feel this is referring to all believers rather than just those who have been heavenly-minded, but in either case, God rewards a longing for the return of Christ.

The *crown of life* refers specifically to those who have suffered greatly for their faith. "Blessed is the man who remains steadfast under trial, for when he has stood the test he will receive the crown of life, which God has promised to those who love him" (Jas 1:12). "Do not fear what you are about to suffer. Behold, the devil is about to throw some of you into prison, that you may be tested, and for ten days you will have tribulation. Be faithful unto death, and I will give you the crown of life" (Rev 2:10).

Finally, we are told of the *crown of glory*, specific to the faithful shepherds of the church. "Shepherd the flock of God that is among you, exercising oversight, not under compulsion, but willingly, as God would have you; not for shameful gain, but eagerly; not domineering over those in your charge, but being examples to the flock. And when the chief Shepherd appears, you will receive the unfading crown of glory" (1 Pet 5:2-4).

We could also highlight a couple other types of rewards: responsibilities and return of losses. In the parable of the minas in Luke 19, Jesus tells the story of a nobleman, speaking here of Himself, who traveled to a far country to receive for himself a kingdom before returning. The nobleman gave ten servants one mina each, which was approximately three month's wages, to be used for kingdom purposes. The faithful servants who multiplied resources on their master's behalf received as their reward the *responsibility* to rule cities. This fits exactly with the reward given to the saints of God in Revelation 22:5 that "they will reign forever and ever."

Another kind of reward is the *return of earthly losses*. In Matthew 19:29, Jesus tells his disciples, "And everyone who has left houses or brothers or sisters or father or mother or children or lands, for my name's sake, will receive a hundredfold and will inherit eternal life." We don't know precisely what He meant but we do know that whatever is lost for the sake of Christ will be repaid at a ridiculous rate of return.

This is only a sample of what Scripture says, as there is so much more described regarding heavenly inheritance, a new heaven and new earth, the wealth of the nations in Revelation 21, and New Jerusalem. Needless to say, heavenly treasure is bigger, better, bolder, and more impenetrable and imperishable than we could ever imagine!

When Do We Receive Our Treasure in Heaven?

The false teacher Kenneth Copeland is famous for teaching that one can make withdrawals on his heavenly treasure while here on earth. This is why, in Copeland's opinion, every Christian should be wealthy on earth. But this is characterizing exactly what Jesus said *not* to do. First Corinthians 3 explains when we will receive our treasure.

> For no one can lay a foundation other than that which is laid, which is Jesus Christ. Now if anyone builds on the foundation with gold, silver, precious stones, wood, hay, straw—each one's work will become manifest, for the Day will disclose it, because it will be revealed by fire, and the fire will test what sort of work each one has done. If the work that anyone has built on the foundation survives, he will receive a reward. (1 Cor 3:11-14)

The good deeds and sacrifices of the saints are characterized metaphorically as building materials, constructed on the foundation of Christ and salvation by grace through faith alone, not by works. They are solid and fireproof; any works that survive God's judgment—those done for the cause of Christ in obedience to His Word with a right heart attitude—will result in reward. Obeying the commands of the Lord, whether that is a husband loving his wife or a wife loving her husband or children obeying their parents or someone giving generously from personal resources—this all results in kingdom reward!

Now, the reward Jesus speaks of is *not* automatic to all believers. Consider the context of 1 Corinthians 3:15, "If anyone's work is burned up, he will suffer loss, though he himself will be saved, but only as through fire." But Paul goes further than to merely speak of your personal choices and priorities. The pronoun "you" in the next two verses are all plural, meaning the group of believers, not just individuals. "Do *you* [plural] not know that *you* are God's temple and that God's Spirit dwells in *you*? If anyone destroys God's temple, God will destroy him. For God's temple is holy, and *you* are that temple" (1 Cor 3:16-17, emphasis added). The building materials on the foundation of Christ are performed, given, and sacrificed in the context of the group effort of the church. We are not to be lone-wolf Christians who think we'll do a mighty work for God independent of our relationship to the local church.

To return to our question, when do we receive our reward? Verse 13 says on "the Day," meaning the end of the age. In all likelihood, this is speaking of sometime after the believers' rapture and resurrection but before the return of Christ.

How Do We Receive Our Treasure in Heaven?

The Apostle Paul instructs Timothy in Ephesus concerning how to lead the church which Timothy pastors, and he gives specific details regarding how to instruct those with material wealth. Interestingly, his directive is very reminiscent of the words of Christ in Matthew 6. Paul writes, "As for the rich in this present age, charge them not to be haughty, nor to set their hopes on the uncertainty of riches, but on God, who richly provides us with everything to enjoy" (1 Tim 6:17). To phrase it as Jesus does, "Do not lay up treasures on earth," expressed as not being haughty or arrogant about one's possessions. Instead, as described in verse 18, "They are to do good, to be rich in good works, to be generous and ready to share." And the result? "Thus storing up treasure for themselves as a good foundation for the future, so that they may take hold of that which is truly life" (v.19).

How do we obtain this reward in relation to financial giving? It happens in the context of the church, to "do good . . . be rich in good works . . . be generous . . . be ready to share." Broadly, this applies to everyone, as the level of our generosity is simply measured by what we have available and can make available to give.

Looking once again at Matthew 6, Jesus summarizes the two questions we've examined: Is your treasure on earth, or is it in heaven? He says, "For where your treasure is, there your heart will be also" (v.21). Jesus gets quite personal as He shifts from using plural pronouns in verses 19–20 to pointing the finger and using singular pronouns to individuals. "For where *your* treasure is, there *your* heart will be also."

An important interpretive question now must be considered. Is Jesus saying, "Give in order to change your heart" or is He saying, "Give because your heart is changed"? In looking at the bigger context, it must be the latter answer. A few verses later, He says, "No one can serve two masters, for either he will hate the one and love the other, or he will be devoted to the one and despise the other. You cannot serve God and money" (6:24). If you refuse to part with even a little of your wealth for the sake of the gospel ministry, then you likely don't belong to Christ.

Spiritual heart change that is not accompanied by a change in the use of money and possessions is questionable and probably not genuine. Let's look back at the returning Jewish exiles to see this point proven. When the remnant of Jewish exiles returned to Jerusalem from Babylon, they began turning once again to God's Word and a revival of faith broke out.

> And all the people gathered as one man into the square before the Water Gate. And they told Ezra the scribe to bring the Book of the Law of Moses that the LORD had commanded Israel… And Ezra opened the book in the sight of all the people, for he was above all the people, and as he opened it all the people stood. And Ezra blessed the LORD, the great God, and all the people answered, "Amen, Amen," lifting up their hands. And they bowed their heads and worshiped the LORD with their faces to the ground. (Neh 8:1, 5-6)

The next verse records various teachers of the Scriptures helping people to understand the law, and then we see the response of the people to what they heard.

> They read from the book, from the Law of God, clearly, and they gave the sense, so that the people understood the reading. And Nehemiah, who was the governor, and Ezra the priest and scribe, and the Levites who taught the people said to all the people, "This day is holy to the LORD your God; do not mourn or weep." For all the people wept as they heard the words of the Law. (vv.8-9)

The people were stunned at how they had not obeyed the Lord—this is the heart of repentance and of turning to the Lord in humility. And the leaders encouraged the people, because in repentance you have right relationship with God and *that* is something to celebrate!

> Then he said to them, "Go your way. Eat the fat and drink sweet wine and send portions to anyone who has nothing ready, for this day is holy to our LORD. And do not be grieved, for the joy of the LORD is your strength." So the Levites calmed all the people, saying, "Be quiet, for this day is holy; do not be grieved." And all the people went their way to eat and drink and to send portions and to make great rejoicing, because they had understood the words that were declared to them. (vv.10-12)

Having been convicted of sin, a special day of repentance was now set aside as a day for the nation to officially turn back to the Lord. What joy it must have been for the people to realize God had changed their hearts to be humble, worshipful, and ready to be obedient!

> Now on the twenty-fourth day of this month the people of Israel were assembled with fasting and in sackcloth, and with earth on their heads. And the Israelites separated themselves from all foreigners and stood and confessed their sins and the iniquities of their fathers. And they stood up in their place and read from the Book of the Law of the LORD their God for a quarter of the day; for another quarter of it they made confession and worshiped the LORD their God. (9:1-3)

The rest of the chapter is a long confession of sin and acknowledgment that they deserved God's discipline because they had turned away from Him. Then they do something stunning — they renew their loyalty to the Lord in writing and list, by name, all who sign this covenant. "Because of all this we make a firm covenant in writing; on the sealed document are the names of our princes, our Levites, and our priests" (9:38). *And guess what else changes because of their heart change?* How they will use their money! Nehemiah 10:32-38 gives a detailed explanation of how the people intended to keep the law of God. As we've stated before, we are not under this same covenant today, but the heart principle is very much the same. A changed heart means our resources will get diverted.

What were the Israelites supporting? Not only were they pledging to contribute to a theocratic, God-ruled government, but also to the service of worship. Verse 39 lists those who were to be supported financially — the priests who minister, the singers, the gatekeepers and administrative staff — to the end that "We will not neglect the house of our God"!

Jesus preached a simple heart test: Is your treasure on earth or in heaven? He Himself took and passed this test with flying colors after His baptism when He was led by the Holy Spirit into the wilderness. Satan was the instrument of the test, or temptation, but there was never any doubt that Jesus would pass and that it would reveal and prove His divine and impeccable nature.

> Again, the devil took him to a very high mountain and showed him all the kingdoms of the world and their glory. And he said to him, "All these I will give you, if you will fall down and worship me." Then Jesus said to him, "Be gone, Satan! For it is written, 'You shall worship the Lord your God and him only shall you serve.'" (Matt 4:8-10)

What was Satan really trying to do? He was trying to tempt Jesus to avoid the cross—to avoid the means by which the wrath of God could be satisfied in order to offer salvation to you and me. "Just rule the world now! Take the wealth of the world now!" But Jesus kept His eyes on the mission given to Him by His Father and was obedient. Hebrews 12:2 says, "for the joy that was set before him endured the cross, despising the shame, and is seated at the right hand of the throne of God." The joy set before Him is further described in Philippians 2:8-11.

> And being found in human form, he humbled himself by becoming obedient to the point of death, even death on a cross. Therefore God has highly exalted him and bestowed on him the name that is above every name, so that at the name of Jesus every knee should bow, in heaven and on earth and under the earth, and every tongue confess that Jesus Christ is Lord, to the glory of God the Father.

To receive this reward, the writer of Hebrews says that Jesus "endured" the cross; this can mean He remained or stayed the course. Remember, Jesus told Peter He could have called upon 72,000 angels to rescue Him if He had wanted! Jesus also "despised the shame," which could mean scorning or showing contempt toward something. However, the most helpful way to define this term is "to think little of something." It's the idea of Jesus receiving and enduring the humiliation and the shame of the cross by thinking little of it in comparison to the rewards for staying the course.

Paul expresses this same idea in Romans 8:18, "For I consider that the sufferings of this present time are not worth comparing with the glory that is to be revealed to us." Basically, "Instead of earthly joy which was within his grasp, Jesus endured the cross and thus obtained greater joy in heaven."[14] Jesus, the Maker of all things, refused the opportunity to immediately receive all that already belonged to Him. Jesus, the Designer of all trees, was crucified on a cross made from a tree He Himself grew. Jesus, the Creator of all humanity, was arrested and murdered by men He Himself created. Any time we're tempted to think we're giving too much for the sake of heavenly reward, we will *never* come close to Christ!

The Lord Jesus lived His heavenly priorities, and He has received a kingdom as a result. We as believers have received kingdom citizenship and the status of fellow heirs with Christ because *He* was faithful unto death. And in all likelihood, none of us will be asked to give what so many other believers have given.

Considering Those Who Have Gone Before Us

Under the cruel reign of Queen Mary, known as "Bloody Mary," Hugh Latimer and Nicholas Ridley were burned at the stake on October 16th, 1555 in Oxford, England. Having both been arrested for treason, defined in this case as believing and preaching the biblical doctrines of grace, the two men shared a cell in the Tower of London for over a year before their deaths. Strong tradition says that as the flames were kindled, Latimer encouraged Ridley, "Be of good comfort, Master Ridley, and play the man; we shall this day light a candle by God's grace in England as shall never be put out."[15]

On November 15th, 1558, five believers in Christ were arrested in Canterbury, Kent, England for believing the genuine gospel contrary to the Catholic religion, and they would become the final martyrs under "Bloody Mary's" rule. Two days later, these five Christians—John Corneford, Christopher Brown, John Herst, Alice Snoth, and Katherine Knight—were burned alive and met the Lord. Before dying yet while tied to the stake, Alice Snoth was allowed to speak to her family, and she proclaimed Christ to her father and grandfather, pleading with them to come to faith. As the flames engulfed her in utter agony, the crowd heard her crying out that she was a follower of Jesus Christ. Joining them in those same years of the English Reformation, executed by Queen Mary, were more—John Rogers, Lawrence Saunders, John Hooper, Rowland Taylor, Rawlins White, Thomas Tompkins, Thomas Causton, Thomas Higbed, William Hunter, Stephen Knight, William Pygot, William Dighel, John Lawrence, Robert Ferrar, George Marsh, William Flower, John Cardmaker, John Warne, Thomas Hawkes, Thomas Watts, John Ardeley, John Simson, Nicholas Chamberlain, William Bamford, Thomas Ormond, John Bradford, John Leaf, John Bland, and countless others—*all burned to death for their faith in Christ*.[16]

These men and women knew where they had stored their treasure. I highly doubt any of them had questions or concerns about giving to the local church body, because now they have become kings and queens in the kingdom of heaven with a vast treasure, a vast reward! You may never be faced with the opportunity to lose your life for Christ, but the opportunity to gain reward for yourself in heaven by your generous, sacrificial giving to the cause of the gospel *is* before you. This opportunity, in fact, is commanded by the Lord: *lay up treasure in heaven.*

Chapter 7

Give Because of God's Glory

I am the pastor of an independent church, meaning we are not attached to any denomination or larger governing body. This has great advantages in many ways but can also present some inherent challenges, especially when it comes to how to properly view a church facility. Independent local churches can at times suffer from tunnel vision when it comes to a facility, meaning that the usefulness and importance of a facility can be undervalued or even viewed with suspicion.[17] Members of independent churches may have qualms, uncertainties, reservations, or misgivings about the pursuit of a useful and helpful facility. I'd like to suggest ten reasons for this phenomenon.

First, independent churches might lack clear examples, being isolated from like-minded churches. One of the benefits of denominations or church associations, which may or may not have a ruling hierarchy, comes in the form of churches setting an example for one another. So, when a local church sets out to improve its facility situation, it has many prior precedents and even people outside the local church to give wisdom and counsel.

Second, independent churches might be suspicious of empty religion, as represented by elaborate church buildings. Early in the days of Protestantism, at the time of the Reformation, there was often pushback against the idea of a cathedral, since good-works salvation theology and empty rituals represented Roman Catholicism. Many well-meaning reformers were rightly concerned about the Catholic pride in cathedrals, so some groups went the opposite direction and insisted that worship be held in plain rooms with four plain walls. Yet this cannot ensure right hearts of worship. In the early to mid-20th century, when many Bible churches began springing up, focusing on verse-by-verse exposition and sound doctrine, some of them historically espoused the idea that a worship space should be plain and cheap. Pews and hymnals, suits and ties — these things were seen as representative of the old and dead and were thus abandoned for the sake of being casual. The pride in formality of the church was replaced with pride of informality and plainness.

A third uncertainty is revealed in one's understanding of end-times. Jesus predicted that His second coming will be like the days of Noah, with people in rebellion and a world of chaotic sin when He suddenly returns. In Revelation, the coming judgments on earth are described — 100-pound hailstones, earthquakes, meteors — and it's tempting to think, "Why spend millions of dollars on a building that a well-timed rock from heaven will likely crush?" But taken to the logical conclusion, people would become like the Millerites of the 1840's who sold everything and climbed into trees to wait for Jesus' return.

Fourth, the seeker sensitive movement has at times ruined the idea of a sacred space. The argument given is that a church facility shouldn't look like a church — it certainly shouldn't have an old-school steeple or stained-glass windows, but rather it should portray a modern, eclectic feel because that's what "the community needs." One writer wrote, "Would you like your doctor to use leeches and other medical 'technology' of a few hundred years ago to treat you today?"[18] Things like steeples and stained-glass windows aren't inherently right or wrong, but this does not mean sacred space for worship is unimportant. Furthermore, this idea presented by that author incorrectly assumes that people will come to faith in Christ because of the building's aesthetics.

Fifth, people may have misgivings about improving church buildings because the right understanding of the indwelling of the Holy Spirit can inadvertently minimize the importance of a sacred space. After all, we don't have to go to a *place* to meet with God; He is with us wherever we go. In fact, the same crowd that misuses this idea often misinterprets Matthew 18:20, "For where two or three are gathered in my name, there am I among them." They take this to mean that they can "do church anywhere," even though the context of the verse concerns a time when the local church needs to confront someone about serious sin. The passage is *not* about "doing church" wherever we please. But again, we see the logical conclusion of that thinking in far too many professing Christians who arrogantly claim, "I don't need to be part of a local church; I can do church on my own or how I want." Yes, we are indwelt by the Holy Spirit and yes, we could technically gather under a big tree and call it our church, but that is clearly not the pattern we see in Scripture.

Sixth, we have been victimized by an overly romanticized idea of informality and spontaneity in worship. People have come to believe that an out-of-tune guitar is more spiritual than a choir, band, or orchestra—that the word "sermon" is too harsh and old-fashioned and we should call it a "message" or "teaching"—that the music is meant to give you a feeling of some sort, instead of being meant to draw your affections heavenward as an offering to God as you receive His attributes—that worship is something you do as a spectator with a latte. And because of this romanticized notion of worship, the independent church can at times place a low value on a worship *space* which promotes excellence and planning and intentionality.

A seventh reason independent churches may have facility challenges concerns the cultural backlash that décor in a church building is somehow a waste of money. We are content to spend thousands of dollars decorating our homes, but we may self-righteously boast that we should save money on the church building. In looking back at ancient Israel, the people often lived in houses made of mud bricks, yet they went to worship God in a temple overlaid with *gold*—their worship facility reflected Who was most important in their lives!

An eighth reason for church building hesitations involves a presupposition or assumption that architecture doesn't or shouldn't matter. But the tabernacle and temple were designed using architecture as a tool to inform the worshiper of God's greatness. From the outside curtains to the inside courtyard where sacrifices were made, even to the Holy Place and the Most Holy Place—these structures and design elements were meant to be tall, elaborate, and overwhelming. God was bigger and more grand that the Israelites, and they humbly recognized their smallness before Him when they approached to worship. Yes, dead worship by false believers can happen in an ornate and beautiful church building, but this can happen in every church building to one degree or another. Jesus promised there would be weeds and tares among the wheat, and that the church would contain frauds. But this shouldn't be a deterrent in creating beauty in our place of worship.

Ninth, many have overused the slogan, "The church is not a building." The church is, of course, defined as all the saved in Christ, those living on earth and those living in heaven. But slogan theology is dangerous because it makes too many assumptions and has too broad of an application. We could also say, "Israel is not a building," but God Himself prescribed that they have a building in which to worship Him.

Finally, the theology of sacred space has suffered from lack of use and review. In our efforts to be spiritual, we can sometimes become platonic in our thinking. Plato's philosophy in basic form asserted that *all* physical things are evil and only the immaterial and spiritual is good; from this view, we begin to devalue the physical, thinking that somehow this is more spiritual. Where we meet together doesn't matter; how you present yourself doesn't matter; what you give to the church doesn't matter. In fact, in this line of thought, the more informal and loose and culturally relevant, the better for our church. But when God met Moses in the burning bush, he told Moses to take off his sandals because the ground was *holy*. It was *sacred space* because God met with Moses there. In other words, do not take lightly that you are meeting with God!

If sacred space were not important, why did Jesus become violently angry when the temple was being misused? He told the moneychangers, "My house shall be called a *house of prayer*" (Matt 21:13, emphasis added). In other words, it was sacred space.

A Sacred Space is a Scriptural Normality

The very first sacred space was in the Garden of Eden, or to be more accurate, the Garden in the land of Eden. This Garden had many similarities with the later-built temple of God because they served the same function, the most crucial being that this sacred space was where God met with mankind. The Garden in Eden was a perfect environment, planted by God Himself, inclusive of all kinds of plants, flowers, and trees that were both beautiful and good for food (Gen 2:9). How do we know this was sacred space? Because when Adam sinned and his communion with God was broken, he was evicted from this place. The *unsacred* was banned from the *sacred*.

We see another example in Old Testament altars and shrines. God would show His grace as the kingdom plan continued forward, and we see mankind continuing to meet with God in lesser sacred spaces which were still considered holy places. This does not imply God is not omnipresent but rather that the identification of a specific place to meet God provided a more tangible understanding of the weightiness and importance of what it meant to commune with the holy God of creation.

Genesis 4 records that Cain and Abel, the sons of Adam and Eve, brought their offerings to the Lord. They went somewhere to present these gifts to the Lord, implying there had to be an altar on which to sacrifice them (at least in Abel's case as he brought animal sacrifices). Genesis 8 describes Noah building an altar to sacrifice to the Lord after safely arriving on the new, post-Flood world. This altar was the first thing Noah built when he disembarked from the ark. When Abram first arrived in Canaan after obeying the call to leave his homeland, God made a covenant with Abram and appeared to him in visible form as a physical manifestation of God. "Then the LORD appeared to Abram and said, "To your offspring I will give this land." So he built there an altar to the LORD, who had appeared to him" (Gen 12:7). More than 500 years after Abram built his altar in Shechem, Joshua gathered Israel together there as well. It was a holy, sacred space because Abram had built an altar to God in that place.

After Abram's sacrifice to God, he made another altar in Bethel and again revisited Bethel to worship the Lord after returning from Egypt. Abraham's grandson Jacob, on his way to Haran as a young man, rested at Bethel, and it was there that he saw the vision of the ladder to heaven. When Jacob awakened, he said, "'Surely the LORD is in this place...' And he was afraid and said, 'How awesome is this place! This is none other than the house of God, and this is the gate of heaven'" (28:16-17). Jacob, too, built a pillar there to commemorate this space as the house of God, which is what the name Bethel means (28:22). Many years later, when Jacob was returning from Haran, he stopped once again at Bethel, and it was here that God changed his name to Israel; God reiterated that Jacob would sire a nation and give rise to kings, and Jacob's response was to erect another stone pillar and pour a drink offering and oil unto the Lord.

A third sacred space shown in the Bible is the tabernacle of Israel — a traveling worship center. Exodus 26 tells us it was constructed of ten massive curtains of fine linen made of blue, purple, and scarlet yarns. The curtains were embroidered with cherubim — angels who are always at God's throne — and the clasps to hold the curtains together were made of gold. Goat's hair was used for a covering for the tent, connected by additional gold clasps. The frames were fashioned out of acacia wood, which was much harder than oak and other woods, and had bases of silver. And that was just the outside! God gives so much ornate detail about every part of this structure, and this was only the traveling version of what was to follow.

Fourth, we see the temple of Jerusalem as a sacred space. Prepared by King David, who raised and donated massive funds for the project, the temple was later built by his son Solomon. Eugene Merrill notes that the Solomonic temple was "a structure that by its very beauty, massiveness, and durability seemed much more suitable to the everlasting God and his presence among his people than the temporality suggested by a mere tent."[19]

Solomon's temple stood grand and awe-inspiring. The inside ceiling measured 180 feet long, 90 feet wide, 50 feet high, and the highest point on the temple was about 20 stories high. It was built with massive stones prepared at the quarry so that the temple area wouldn't be polluted by the sounds of hammers and other tools working on the site. Inner sanctuary floors, walls, and ceilings were made of cypress and cedar, and carved gourds and blossoming flowers embellished the cedar.

The innermost sanctuary was a cube, 30 feet high, wide, and long, and was completely overlaid with gold — that's 5,400 square feet of gold surface area! In this innermost Holy of Holies space were two cherubim angels made of olive wood, each 15 feet high with a wingspan of 15 feet. All around the walls were carved angels, palm trees, and flowers, and the outer part of the building was decorated with carved pomegranates. These were reminders to Israel of paradise lost, the first sacred space: *The Garden of Eden!* The temple symbolized hope for paradise regained someday. And when the finished temple was dedicated, the priests of God went into the Holy Place for dedication as well. And what a worship service they had!

> And when the priests came out of the Holy Place (for all the priests who were present had consecrated themselves, without regard to their divisions, and all the Levitical singers, Asaph, Heman, and Jeduthun, their sons and kinsmen, arrayed in fine linen, with cymbals, harps, and lyres, stood east of the altar with 120 priests who were trumpeters; and it was the duty of the trumpeters and singers to make themselves heard in unison in praise and thanksgiving to the LORD), and when the song was raised, with trumpets and cymbals and other musical instruments, in praise to the LORD, "For he is good, for his steadfast love endures forever," the house, the house of the LORD, was filled with a cloud, so that the priests could not stand to minister because of the cloud, for the glory of the LORD filled the house of God. (2 Chron 5:11–14)

That is sacred space taken to glorious levels!

In the New Testament, under the New Covenant in Christ, where did the church want to gather? They also met at the temple because they were worshiping the same God, but now as New Covenant followers of Christ. The new church in Jerusalem gathered in the outer courts of the temple by the thousands. But great persecution, beginning with the stoning of Stephen and resulting in the dispersion of many Jerusalem Christians, made meeting at the temple difficult. Christians often tried to use Jewish synagogues for their worship spaces, such as the time Paul proclaimed the gospel to Jews in Ephesus. Yet he encountered great opposition, and the true believers had to follow him out of the synagogue to the Hall of Tyrannus, most likely a lecture hall or school. The church of Corinth met in the home of Philemon to worship (Phlm 1) and the church at Laodicea congregated in the house of Nympha (Col 4:15). The church in Rome, or at least part of it, worshiped in the house of Priscilla and Aquila (Rom 16:3-5).

For a long time, the church of Jesus Christ had no sacred space, and when persecution became extremely deadly under the reign of Nero and his successors, having an official sacred space anywhere in the Roman Empire became virtually impossible. But in the fourth century when persecution abated, one of the first things the church began doing was erecting church buildings — getting back to having a sacred space devoted to the worship of God in Christ. A sacred space is a Scriptural *normality*.

A Sacred Space is a Financial Priority

In Exodus, God had just rescued Israel from bondage in Egypt, He had just given them the Israelite Covenant (more commonly called the Mosaic Covenant) represented by the Ten Commandments, and Israel had agreed to follow the Lord their God and serve only Him because of His great love for them. Almost immediately, God begins to delineate sacred space.

The Israelites had plundered the Egyptians when, by God's sovereign power, the Egyptians willingly gave them great wealth, and now we see the purpose of these possessions.

> The LORD said to Moses, "Speak to the people of Israel, that they take for me a contribution. From every man whose heart moves him you shall receive the contribution for me. And this is the contribution that you shall receive from them: gold, silver, and bronze, blue and purple and scarlet yarns and fine twined linen, goats' hair, tanned rams' skins, goatskins, acacia wood, oil for the lamps, spices for the anointing oil and for the fragrant incense, onyx stones, and stones for setting, for the ephod and for the breastpiece. And let them make me a sanctuary, that I may dwell in their midst. Exactly as I show you concerning the pattern of the tabernacle, and of all its furniture, so you shall make it. (Ex 25:1-9)

Verse 8 provides the reason for this structure they were to build, "that I may dwell in their midst." This was to be the place that God would meet with mankind on earth, and the context demonstrates the importance of this place.

> On the third new moon after the people of Israel had gone out of the land of Egypt, on that day they came into the wilderness of Sinai... On the morning of the third day there were thunders and lightnings and a thick cloud on the mountain and a very loud trumpet blast, so that all the people in the camp trembled. Then Moses brought the people out of the camp to meet God, and they took their stand at the foot of the mountain. Now Mount Sinai was wrapped in smoke because the LORD had descended on it in fire. The smoke of it went up like the smoke of a kiln, and the whole mountain trembled greatly. And as the sound of the trumpet grew louder and louder, Moses spoke, and God answered him in thunder. The LORD came down on Mount Sinai, to the top of the mountain. And the LORD called Moses to the top of the mountain, and Moses went up. (19:1,16-20)

Moses is on Mount Sinai, meeting with God on behalf of Israel. It might have been tempting on the part of the people to try to see God, but He warns in 19:21-22, "And the LORD said to Moses, 'Go down and warn the people, lest they break through to the LORD to look and many of them perish. Also let the priests who come near to the LORD consecrate themselves, lest the LORD break out against them.'" In other words, you don't get to meet with God anytime, anyplace, and in any fashion you want. In the next chapter, God spoke to Moses and presented him with the Ten Commandments, the covenant God was making with His people.

Following this episode, several chapters give preliminary laws for how the covenant was to be worked out and lived in society. And now the people have a choice to make: will they agree to the covenant God has laid out for them? "Moses came and told the people all the words of the LORD and all the rules. And all the people answered with one voice and said, 'All the words that the LORD has spoken we will do. And Moses wrote down all the words of the LORD'" (24:3-4a).

Moses has written a copy of the law, and the people choose to agree to it. He is then called back up the mountain to receive the tablets of stone containing God's written word—ten commandments on each of the two tablets, one for Israel and one for God, as was the Ancient Near East custom of making a copy of the covenant for each party. Moses would stay on the mountain for forty days and forty nights (24:17-18). What might be the first thing God tells Moses on Mount Sinai? He makes absolutely clear the importance of His holiness and the ability to rightly meet with Him. "The LORD said to Moses, 'Speak to the people of Israel, that they take for me a *contribution*. From every man whose heart moves him you shall receive the *contribution* for me'" (25:1-2, emphasis added). From chapter 25 until chapter 31, God explains specific details for the ornate, intricately-designed tabernacle. In one of the greatest moments in human history, "And he gave to Moses, when he had finished speaking with him on Mount Sinai, the two tablets of the testimony, tablets of stone, written with the finger of God" (31:18).

Remember the very first instruction God had commanded Moses concerning how God's people could meet with Him? They had been told to take a contribution of their wealth to build a sanctuary to rightly meet with the living God. But even as Moses meets with God on the mountain, what were the people doing down below? They were *violating* the first and second commandments they had just agreed to, and instead they make a golden calf image that supposedly represented God!

Since God's people broke God's covenant, Moses shatters the two tablets, in essence "tearing up" the contract the Lord had so graciously made with them. God disciplines Israel severely when 3,000 men die by the sword at His command. And then God stuns both Moses and the people by telling them to go to the land He promised them, but *He would not go with them.* "When the people heard this disastrous word, they mourned" (33:4). Immediately, Moses intercedes on behalf of the people, appealing to God on the basis of God's own glory.

> And he said to him, "If your presence will not go with me, do not bring us up from here. For how shall it be known that I have found favor in your sight, I and your people? Is it not in your going with us, so that we are distinct, I and your people, from every other people on the face of the earth?" And the LORD said to Moses, "This very thing that you have spoken I will do, for you have found favor in my sight, and I know you by name." (33:15-17)

Moses then requests to see the glory of God as confirmation that God would be with Israel. He ascends the mountain yet again to receive two new tablets, and God shows His glory to Moses by proclaiming words of His great glory in continuing as Israel's God.

> The LORD passed before him and proclaimed, "The LORD, the LORD, a God merciful and gracious, slow to anger, and abounding in steadfast love and faithfulness, keeping steadfast love for thousands, forgiving iniquity and

transgression and sin, but who will by no means clear the guilty, visiting the iniquity of the fathers on the children and the children's children, to the third and the fourth generation." And Moses quickly bowed his head toward the earth and worshiped. And he said, "If now I have found favor in your sight, O LORD, please let the LORD go in the midst of us, for it is a stiff-necked people, and pardon our iniquity and our sin, and take us for your inheritance." (34:6-9)

In *all this drama*, God's priority for Israel never changed. When Moses first went up Mount Sinai, God told him to take a *contribution* from the people of Israel. Meanwhile, the people disobeyed and were disciplined; now, Moses receives a second copy of the tablets and comes back to the people, exhorting them, "Whoever is of a generous heart, let him bring the LORD's *contribution*" (35:5, emphasis added). God had killed the worst offenders concerning the golden calf image, and He had threatened to abandon His people because of their sin; they had very narrowly missed the wrath of God. He was not looking for mere external obedience; God required a right *heart* of worship—a tender, yielded, humble, and submissive heart, as demonstrated in the response of the people. Notice what is important to God!

> And they came, everyone whose *heart* stirred him, and everyone whose spirit moved him, and brought the LORD's contribution to be used for the tent of meeting, and for all its service, and for the holy garments. So they came, both men and women. All who were of a *willing heart* brought brooches and earrings and signet rings and armlets, all sorts of gold objects, every man dedicating an offering of gold to the LORD. And every one who possessed blue or purple or scarlet yarns or fine linen or goats' hair or tanned rams' skins or goatskins brought them. Everyone who could make a contribution of silver or bronze brought it as the LORD's contribution. And every one who possessed acacia wood of any use in the work brought it. And every skillful woman spun with her hands, and they all brought what they had

spun in blue and purple and scarlet yarns and fine twined linen. All the women whose *hearts* stirred them to use their skill spun the goats' hair. And the leaders brought onyx stones and stones to be set, for the ephod and for the breastpiece, and spices and oil for the light, and for the anointing oil, and for the fragrant incense. All the men and women, the people of Israel, whose *heart* moved them to bring anything for the work that the LORD had commanded by Moses to be done brought it as a freewill offering to the LORD. (35:21-29, emphasis added)

But this wasn't just a one-time gift. "And they received from Moses all the contribution that the people of Israel had brought for doing the work on the sanctuary. They still kept bringing him freewill offerings every morning" (36:3). They gave until they had all that was needed!

In the sovereign purposes of God, He used the golden calf incident to soften the people's hearts and to reveal true worshipers. The ones who repented were stirred in their hearts to create a sacred space to meet with their holy, kind, and gracious God who had delivered them from Egypt.

Sacred space was an absolute priority. It was God's idea to give an offering for the building of the sacred space, and the people were to present gifts from the heart. This didn't mean everyone gave *equal* gifts—some gave gold, some bronze, and others gave loving labor constructing the tabernacle. There was an initial gift, the giving was continually offered, and the people gave until the job was done, thus clearly demonstrating the financial priority of a sacred space.

A Sacred Space is a Spiritual Necessity

In Deuteronomy 4:10, Moses reminded Israel that 40 years earlier, God had given them a command. "The LORD said to me, 'Gather the people to me, that I may let them hear my words, so that they may learn to fear me all the days that they live on the earth, and that they may teach their children so.'" In our individualistic, cultural thinking, we generally hear this primarily as a functional command—that the primary reason for the assembly of God's people is to facilitate the hearing of Scripture. The assembly becomes simply a means to that end, because if the Israelites did not congregate together, they couldn't physically hear God's Word.

With the inventions which media technology has provided, developments which God has used for His glory, there *can* exist a negative effect of degrading and lowering the importance of the corporate gathering. Gutenberg's printing press enabled the mass publication of the Bible as well as other books about the Bible, and the need to gather was slightly diminished. Voice recording, handheld devices, the internet, podcasts, social media, and other outlets enable us to listen to the Word of God preached anywhere at any time.

This technological advancement provides an incredible way to spread the gospel, but it also has an unintended impact on the meeting together of believers. Today, people can be part of pseudo-gatherings and some men call themselves "online pastors." If someone doesn't like the churches in his area, he convinces himself So-and-So is his pastor because that's who he tunes in to hear on the radio or podcast. But this is *not* what God intended!

So why do we gather? Why don't we simply establish various tiny Bible studies around the community? First, gathering and meeting together is a foretaste of the time all of redeemed humanity will gather together, and both the biblical scenes in heaven and the scenes depicting the return of Christ center on this idea. Second, it is the best way to sing God's praises. Psalm 149:1 says, "Praise the LORD! Sing to the LORD a new song, his praise *in the assembly of the godly!*" (emphasis added). Third, it creates a common bond and keeps unlikely people together. The church of Jesus Christ is comprised of the saved rather than particular social, ethnic, or economic groups.

Fourth, gathering together builds up the body of Christ. Paul told the elders of the Ephesian church, "And now I commend you to God and to the word of his grace, which is able to build you up and to give you the inheritance among all those who are sanctified" (Acts 20:32). The word of His grace in this context seems to be speaking of the assembling of Christians who desire to hear God's Word read and preached. And fifth, it proclaims the identity of those who love Christ, in contrast with those who don't. "They went out from us, but they were not of us; for if they had been of us, they would have continued with us. But they went out, that it might become plain that they all are not of us" (1 John 2:19).

So, with great Scriptural precedent and with great spiritual confidence, we boldly proclaim that sacred space is important. It is a Scriptural normality, a financial priority, and a spiritual necessity. Great things in the church are not accomplished by great people — they are accomplished by weak, dependent people who worship a great God. *Soli Deo Gloria* — For God's glory alone!

Chapter 8

Give Because of God's Kingdom

I have saved what I consider the most exciting and thrilling reason we give: Because of God's kingdom. Revelation 21 is the first chapter in the Bible since Genesis 2 which isn't tainted by sin. All of the elect have been brought into the kingdom, and Christ has finally established His kingdom on earth after the Great Tribulation. After 1,000 years of an age better than our current one (Rev 20:1-6; Zech 14:16-21) but not yet the final state, epic and cosmic things will happen.[20]

Satan and his followers—fallen angels and humans—will be judged and thrown into the lake of fire, and at this judgment "earth and sky fled away" from God's presence (Rev 20:11). Given that Revelation 20 says there is no place for the unsaved to hide, it seems that the great judgment of the rebellious will take place after the melting down of the known creation. Following this judgment, in which the reprobates of all spiritual and physical realms are condemned, we are shown a glorious scene of the future for all who have placed their faith in Christ: "Then I saw a new heaven and a new earth, for the first heaven and the first earth had passed away, and the sea was no more" (21:1).

Creation has been redeemed! The most obvious sign of God's judgment has been removed from the earth—the oceans formed from the Flood of Noah's day. We also receive valuable information about New Jerusalem that is specific to why we should be giving right now. This chapter will make basically one main point about giving, but to give that point depth and meaning, let's simply enjoy a preview of this coming kingdom and take a look at New Jerusalem from far away, close up, and from the inside.

New Jerusalem Far Away

> And I saw the holy city, new Jerusalem, coming down out of heaven from God, prepared as a bride adorned for her husband...Then came one of the seven angels who had the seven bowls full of the seven last plagues and spoke to me, saying, "Come, I will show you the Bride, the wife of the Lamb." And he carried me away in the Spirit to a great, high mountain, and showed me the holy city Jerusalem coming down out of heaven from God. (Rev 21:2, 9-10)

Verses 2 and 10 are describing the same event: New Jerusalem coming down out of heaven. Heaven and earth are now essentially one, and we notice several features from far away in this chapter.

New Jerusalem is a transportable city, a single unit, coming down out of the heavens to New Earth. Given the size and transportable nature of the city, our current set of the laws of physics will not be sufficient to contain it. God will have to do something different, and the materials that comprise the city will have to be of a different sort, since no earthly building material could withstand its own weight at the height and size described in subsequent verses.

New Jerusalem is a brilliant city, having the glory of God and radiating with the very glory of God Himself. Revelation 21:11 says, "having the glory of God, its radiance like a most rare jewel, like a jasper, clear as crystal." The best understanding we have of jasper is that it may represent a diamond. In the next chapter of

Revelation, the glory of God lights up New Jerusalem; the walls are illuminated with the glory of God *from the inside out*!

New Jerusalem is a huge city. "And the one who spoke with me had a measuring rod of gold to measure the city and its gates and walls. The city lies foursquare, its length the same as its width. And he measured the city with his rod, 12,000 stadia. Its length and width and height are equal" (21:15-16). A stadion is about 607 feet, so 12,000 stadia would equal about 1,400 miles in every direction. This is comparable to approximately half of the United States — over 2 million square miles — just on one level! Many feel the city is shaped as a pyramid, but that's not clear in the text. More likely, the city is patterned after the place where God met with men in the temple — the Holy of Holies — which was shaped as a cube. Most certainly the city will contain a variety of levels and they probably won't all be the same. Even if each level were a mile high, that would still be 1,400 levels.

This would necessitate a significantly larger earth, but that's not a problem. In 2012, astronomers spotted a planet thirteen times larger than Jupiter, meaning that on a volume basis, you could fit about 17,173 earths into this "Super-Jupiter" planet.[21] So, from a distance New Jerusalem is like a massive diamond coming out of heaven, brilliantly lighting up everything else around it.

New Jerusalem Close Up

Walls

Usually a wall is meant to keep out enemies, but since there will no longer be any enemies of God, this is purely to display the glory of God. The walls and gate are a testimony that some can come in and most cannot. Verse 12 says the city has "a great, high wall" but doesn't clarify how high. Verse 17 says the wall is 216 feet, but doesn't say whether this is the wall's height or thickness.

Due to the size of the city itself, a wall 216 feet high would be a drop in the bucket, and the cube is an important shape in the Bible, being the exact shape of the Holy of Holies. If that is the case, then perhaps 216 feet refers to the wall's thickness. Yet, verse 18 seems to indicate that John can see the wall as well as the city: "The wall was built of jasper, while the city was pure gold, like clear glass." We also know these are real measurements, not symbolic, since they are measured in human cubits and a detail is added that this is the same as an angelic cubit. This would make no sense if these numbers were purely symbolic.

The reason the city looks like a diamond coming out of the sky is because it *is* a diamond coming out of the sky. "The wall was built of jasper" (21:18), which we determined is most likely diamond. John peeks ahead to see the contrast between the wall and the city itself, and it seems that while the outside is more like a diamond, the inside is more like gold, though the gold is like clear glass.

Gates

The gates to the city each feature a welcoming angel, and the gates are named after the twelve tribes of Israel. This idea celebrates God's faithfulness and covenant relationship with Israel—all the promises and prophecies are now fulfilled! If Israel is gone or missing from the end times, then these gates are no more than gravestones. But they are named after the men and tribes who will one day be on New Earth! Why? Because God chose them—He elected them. "For the LORD has chosen Jacob for himself, Israel as his own possession" (Ps 135:4).

As to the location of the gates, "on the east three gates, on the north three gates, on the south three gates, and on the west three gates" (Rev 21:13). If three gates are on each side of the city, if each side is 1,400 miles long, and if the gates are equidistant from each other, that divides each side into four parts with the gates 350 miles apart from each other. We're not told the size of the gates; but they could feasibly be miles long! And they have the well-known appearance described by John, "The twelve gates were twelve pearls, each of the gates made of a single pearl" (21:21), thus the phrase "the pearly gates."

"And its gates will never be shut by day—and there will be no night there" (21:25). The gates are no longer used for protection, only for entry and exit from New Jerusalem, as well as perhaps the most popular meeting places that believers have arranged here on earth!

Foundations

The foundations (or possibly foundation stones) are also named. "And the wall of the city had twelve foundations, and on them were the twelve names of the twelve apostles of the Lamb" (21:14). Jesus promised the disciples in Matthew 19:28 that "in the new world, when the Son of Man will sit on his glorious throne, you who have followed me will also sit on twelve thrones, judging the twelve tribes of Israel." The foundations seem to be especially ornate in their décor, and we see in Revelation 21:19-20 every kind of jewel: jasper, sapphire, agate, emerald, onyx, carnelian, chrysolite, beryl, topaz, chrysoprase, jacinth, and amethyst.

These jewels roughly parallel the stones worn on the breastplate of the high priest of Israel as described in Exodus 28. Additionally, a more detailed study of these stones would reveal that they are the same colors as the rainbow and in the correct order, beginning with onyx. Abraham looked forward to seeing this city, recorded in Hebrews 11:9-10. "By faith...he was looking forward to the city that has foundations, whose designer and builder is God." So if you can picture foundations adorned with a rainbow of jewels, you're getting close!

New Jerusalem from the Inside

We have looked at New Jerusalem from a far away and a close up perspective, so now let's explore the inside. To do this, we'll first consider some elements that are *not* present.

What's Not Inside

"And I saw no temple in the city, for its temple is the Lord God the Almighty and the Lamb" (Rev 21:22). In the prior chapter, we studied the fact that beginning with the Garden in Eden, God has always had a sacred space where mankind can worship Him. But since God is dwelling among men and has fulfilled this eternal promise, the temple of New Jerusalem is the Lord God, the Almighty, the Lamb! *All space* has now become sacred, and faith has become sight. The need for symbols and mediation are done away with, and now there is complete, constant, direct communication with God face to face. What we used to call prayer is now called a conversation.

There is also no need of sun or moon. The text is specific here, "And the city has no *need* of sun or moon to shine on it, for the glory of God gives it light, and its lamp is the Lamb" (21:23, emphasis added). This is New Earth situated in New Heaven with certainly new stars and most likely a new sun and new moon. But the sun and moon make no contribution to the amount of light shone by the very glory of God. It would be like lighting a candle and holding it in front of a supernova—there is no need!

In the city, "there will be no night there" (21:25), and "night will be no more. They will need no light of lamp or sun, for the Lord God will be their light, and they will reign forever and ever" (22:5). This is not necessarily the permanent eradication of nighttime; the context here is New Jerusalem, which is lit completely by the glory of God, and when God created the world, He pronounced day and night as "very good." Nighttime and darkness became metaphors for sin and evil, but night was never inherently part of the curse of sin—it is in the night sky that we see the glorious cosmos of God's creation! But in the area of New Jerusalem, there is never darkness. God's glory permeates all.

Absent from New Jerusalem will be anything or anyone unclean (21:27) or anything accursed (22:3). This doesn't imply they are right outside the city gates somewhere, but rather it demonstrates the *wholly* and *holy* sinless nature of the new world. For all citizens, access to God is continually unbroken, and it is now too late for those who rejected Christ's free offer of salvation from sin. In New Jerusalem and on New Earth, there is no more curse. All effects of the curse of God on mankind listed in Genesis 3 will be eradicated—the ground is not cursed; there is no more sin or consequences of sin, there is no more death.

What Is Inside

"The street of the city was pure gold, like transparent glass" (Rev 21:21). In our culture, "the streets" tend to have a negative connotation. When a felon is let out of prison early, we say he's back on the streets; a homeless person is said to live on the street. Even in Scripture, the 80-plus references to the street are almost all associated with pain and suffering. For example, Psalm 144:14 says, "may there be no cry of distress in our streets!" and Psalm 18:42 speaks of the "mire of the streets." When Jerusalem was destroyed in 586 BC Jeremiah wrote of young women and men lying dead in the streets (Lam 2:21). Almost every reference to the streets in the Bible is laced with grief and sorrow, although in Zechariah 8, God promises peace that will come to Jerusalem during the prior millennial kingdom. "Thus says the LORD of hosts: Old men and old women shall again sit in the streets of Jerusalem, each with staff in hand because of great age. And the streets of the city shall be full of boys and girls playing in its streets" (Zech 8:4-5).

The street of gold (singular) may possibly be referring to the main street which leads to God's throne. It is pure gold like transparent glass—unfathomable to our limited minds! But think of the important implication of streets of New Jerusalem. These provide access to God, paved in gold! There is the hustle and bustle of glorious New Jerusalem activity. People are on the streets, every person a gloriously perfected saint with whom you can enjoy perfect fellowship. There are avenues to explore the glories of New Jerusalem—there are places to go and people to see!

Only those who have been redeemed by Jesus Christ, the sacrificial Lamb, will have their names written in the Lamb's Book of Life, which will also be in New Jerusalem (Rev 21:27). Furthermore, "They will see his face, and his name will be on their foreheads" (22:4). We don't know precisely what this means, but it has the connotation of being permanently identified with Christ and is likely the unknown name of Christ referenced in Revelation 19:12, "His eyes are like a flame of fire, and on his head are many diadems, and he has a name written that no one knows but himself." This name is also referenced in Christ's exaltation in Philippians 2:9-11, "Therefore God has highly exalted him and bestowed on him the name that is above every name, so that at the name of Jesus every knee should bow, in heaven and on earth and under the earth, and every tongue confess that Jesus Christ is Lord, to the glory of God the Father." Thus, in comparison with Revelation 19:12, it is unlikely that the "name of Jesus" here speaks of the name, "Jesus," but means "the name which *belongs* to Jesus," one which has not yet been revealed. God will unveil a surprise name which belongs to Jesus, expressing His might, His glory, His goodness, and His grace.

Never again will we leave the glorious gathering of the church to be splashed with the mire of a sinful world. Now, everywhere we go in the 2,744,000,000 cubic miles (give or take a few hundred million) of New Jerusalem—you will only and always interact with believers, those with the name of Christ—every single one saved by grace.

Revelation 22:1-2 describes the rivers of the water of life as being "bright as crystal, flowing from the throne of God and of the Lamb through the middle of the street of the city; also, on either side of the river, the tree of life with its twelve kinds of fruit, yielding its fruit each month. The leaves of the tree were for the healing of the nations." In the Bible, rivers and streams are seen as a source of life, a source of cleansing, a place where man encounters God, and an agent of God's rescue. Ancient Israel didn't have much to boast of in the way of rivers, except the Jordan River. There were also wadis—dry creek-beds that ran when it rained. But there are numerous references in the Old Testament to rivers and streams as images of the hope of coming Paradise. Psalm 36:6-7, "How precious is your steadfast love, O God! The children of mankind take refuge in the shadow of your wings. They feast on the abundance of your house, and you give them drink from the river of your delights."

This river of life pictures a return to Eden. In the original Garden of Eden, a main river divided into four rivers, which each flowed from the garden. Also, the river of the water of life is likely not one big gushing torrent down main street. It waters all of New Jerusalem with side streams, certainly highlighted by lovely landscaping and trees. Psalm 46:4 tells us, "There is a river whose streams make glad the city of God, the holy habitation of the Most High," and Isaiah 33:20-21 confirms this as well.

The river of the waters of life flow from the throne of God and of the Lamb. Currently, we are promised access to boldly approach the throne of grace in prayer where we will find mercy and grace to help in time of need (Heb 4:16). But in New Jerusalem we can literally *go to* the throne! We can speak to our God face to face, being in awe of the spectacle of the glory of God and His angels.

And inside the city, the stunning sight of the tree of life captures our attention. It appears for the first time since the Garden of Eden, other than a brief mention in Revelation 2:7 that it is in the current heaven in the "paradise of God." Revelation 22:7 says there is "also, on either side of the river, the tree of life with its twelve kinds of fruit, yielding its fruit each month. The leaves of the tree were for the healing of the nations." Here, the original text doesn't include a definite article ("*the* tree"), so the phrase could be arguably translated as "*a* tree of life on either side of the river." The tree has 12 kinds of fruit that yield produce every month for the healing of the nations. Somehow, the tree is related to the maintenance of eternal life, but the primary emphasis seems to be the peace of the nations for all eternity.

Will we eat in heaven? Yes, but for pleasure, not survival. The church has been deeply harmed by the faulty view of heaven as an ethereal, other-worldly, spooky existence, and this has made even Christians to worry about boredom or a lack of enjoyment. Yet nothing could be further from the truth. We will eat, drink, laugh, sing, play, love, and fellowship — all the best of God's intentions for His creation to enjoy Him and His work will exist in perfected form!

What's Happening Inside

"By its light will the nations walk, and the kings of the earth will bring their glory into it, and its gates will never be shut by day" (Rev 22:24-25). City gates were typically used for protection from enemies, but there are no enemies waiting outside these gates. Each gate is attended by an angel (21:12), and every citizen of New Earth is completely welcome to access the throne of the King. The gates are so far apart that it's entirely likely that every gate exits into a completely different terrain. People will be coming in and out to worship, for pleasure, to perform a task, to bring gifts to the Lord, to attend reunions and banquets, and to just enjoy the city — the possibilities are endless!

In ancient times, the city gate was where the action happened; people gathered together, told stories, and made deals and bargains. The gates will be open, but they will also be a gathering place of reunion and joy and action if the pattern of the Bible is any pattern for the future gates.

Just for perspective, we've said that New Jerusalem could potentially have 2 million square miles on just one level. There is currently about 25 million square miles of habitable space on earth, so if there is a level for each mile, this means there would be a habitable surface area of 112 earths...and this is only New Jerusalem, not counting the rest of New Earth! We can safely say there will be plenty of things to do!

"The throne of God and of the Lamb will be in it, and his servants will worship him" (22:3). Currently, we have to work at undistracted worship, but in New Jerusalem our worship will be undistracted, sheer bliss and pleasure as we give all glory to God. We will receive all ecstasy in the very presence of God Himself, and our worship will be as incredible as New Earth. It will be the highlight and the greatest part of our life there.

Imagine the most awe-inspiring worship service you've ever attended, and this won't even begin to scratch the surface of what worship will be like in New Jerusalem. Psalm 150 says that every instrument, voice, and dance will be utilized in giving praise to God. Picture a choir of a million voices, an orchestra of a million instruments, and tens of thousands of dancing saints and flying angels proclaiming the glory of God! Significantly, Psalm 150 lists the trumpet first, a common way in Scripture to announce, "God is here!"

But notice also the end of Revelation 22:3, "and his servants will worship him." There is a clear connection between God's servants and the fact that they (we) are worshiping Him. The Greek word used for worship here is used interchangeably for the concepts of both worship and service, specifically divine service. As we are commanded to strive for serving now, we will also *serve* the Lord on New Earth and in New Jerusalem as an act of worship.

Jesus taught that an aspect of our heavenly reward will be to take part in the administration of the final state. He gave a preview of the role that governing will hold in the future kingdom (Luke 19:11-27). And Revelation 22 bears this aspect of governing out as well: "And night will be no more. They will need no light of lamp or sun, for the Lord God will be their light, and they will reign forever and ever" (22:5). Apparently, some people will have more responsibility than others, implying activity, interests, and occupations. You will fulfill your God-given purpose as someone created in His image, just as it was originally intended in the Garden of Eden that mankind have dominion over the earth (Gen 1:26-28). On New Earth, it's as if God will say to mankind, "Welcome back to Eden! Let's pick up where we left off — I created you to rule the earth with Me!"

The One Point about Giving

And now, at last, we get valuable information about New Jerusalem specific to why we should be giving *right now*. How does this look at New Jerusalem tell us we should be giving faithfully? *Because you will **always** be giving to the Lord!*

Giving is an eternal activity! Revelation 21:24-26 tell us that the kings of the earth will bring their glory and honor to New Jerusalem. This Greek word translated "honor" is often used in the New Testament to speak of money and wealth (e.g., Matt 27:6; Acts 5:2; 7:6; 19:19; 1 Tim 5:17). The kings of the earth cannot be said to simply be bringing in to New Jerusalem *ideas* or *concepts* of "glory and honor." They are *carrying something*. The end times shows us a scene of the kings of the earth bringing the glorious riches of their lands—their goods and products—as some sort of commerce, first as a gift to the *Lord*.

Even in the millennial kingdom, we learn in Zechariah 14:14, "And the wealth of all the surrounding nations shall be collected, gold, silver, and garments in great abundance." Also in the millennial kingdom, Isaiah 60:11-12 says, "Your gates shall be open continually; day and night they shall not be shut, that people may bring to you the wealth of the nations, with their kings led in procession." If this is the pattern, then we can picture great and grand parades of the wealth and treasure being triumphantly marched into New Jerusalem! The nations will be like the Queen of Sheba in Solomon's day bringing to the king gold, spices, precious stones, wood, and musical instruments (1 Kgs 10).

Where will all this wealth originate, brought as a glorious offering of love to the King of kings *by* all the kings? The only viable option is that the wealth with be *given and collected* to be brought to New Jerusalem. What joy we will have to be able to give of our great abundance toward a massive, nationwide offering to the Lord!

The Most Important Gift of All

But you can *only* be a part of this joy if you are found in Christ—if you have repented of your sin, which keeps you from fellowship with God—if you trust that Christ alone paid the penalty of your countless offenses against God. If you desire to be part of this glorious kingdom, in which you can give freely unto the Lord, He must first *give you* salvation in Christ by His grace alone through your faith alone. You can offer nothing to merit this salvation; it is the gift of God. Then and only then can you be part of the kingdom.

When I was 14 years old, I was given the opportunity to participate in something that has now become a fond memory—marching in the Rose Parade on New Year's Day in Pasadena, California. I can still remember the adrenaline and the excitement of all the bands and the floats and the millions of roses everywhere, even the Grand Marshal—world-famous actor Jimmy Stewart—riding in an open car. Well, the grand parade in New Jerusalem will eclipse the little, tiny parades we create on this earth! Isaiah 60 says that people— *you*—will bring the wealth of the nations with their kings in procession. You will march through the gates of pearl, through the diamond walls onto the streets of gold, alongside the river of life under the tree of life, to give to the Lord seated on His throne!

You will give in gratitude for the cross of Christ, upon which our Savior suffered. You will give in gratitude for the cross of Christ, upon which your sins were obliterated. You will give in gratitude for the cross of Christ, through which your eternal destiny with God was purchased. And you will give in gratitude for the cross of Christ, which should have been *your* cross for your *own* iniquity.

The offering you present to the Lord in New Jerusalem will be your thanks and gratitude for the cross which purchased your freedom from sin and entrance into this glorious eternal kingdom. I hope and pray, that based upon your *eternal* act of giving, you will exhibit here on this earth *joyful generosity*, for this is your rightful response to God's grace.

Appendix:
Our Rationale for a Capital Campaign

To be very clear, the following is not a generic template as to why any and every local church might pursue a capital campaign for a more permanent facility. This is simply what our elders in our unique circumstances concluded. Perhaps you might resonate with some of these reasons in your own situation. The following represents a condensed version of our rationale:

1. ***Stop paying rent.*** We believed it was incumbent upon us to not burden the future membership of the church with a crisis situation if the church could not stay in this current facility due to ownership change or the whims of the current owners. We did not want future members saying, "Why didn't they do something when there was still time?" Additionally, the rent we paid (at the time of this writing) was extremely high, and those funds could be better used toward an owned facility for the same reasons individual families pursue home ownership rather than renting perpetually.

2. *Increase our ability to gather as a whole body.* While some idealists say, "the church isn't a building" — and frankly I don't know a single Christian who actually *believes* that the church *is* a building — the church *does* value the ability to gather all together. The church at Jerusalem in the book of Acts gathered at Solomon's Porch on the temple grounds because they instinctively wanted to gather all together. Historically, churches that are effective for the gospel over the long haul have owned their own land and worship space.

3. *Increase our ability to disciple through preaching and teaching.* As a preacher, I would preach to as many people as God would give. If you were a fisherman, would you rather fish in a pond with a few fish or in a lake *teeming* with fish? This is *not* church growth for its own sake; this is rooted in a desire to proclaim the biblical gospel of grace to as many as possible and to mature in the faith as many believers as possible. Our church leans heavily toward discipleship, including our basics of the faith training and our advanced theology and Bible training we offer all the members. But the space we had for facilitating this was limited, shared with stacked chairs and tables, equipment, cabinets, and other things with no other home. Our main discipleship area was just too small and cramped and not designed to be a dedicated learning space. Lecture and learning space is different than worship space. It needs tabletops, coffee and snack stations, media tools, easy-access restrooms, and all the other helps that enable learning. In addition to those adult discipleship needs, we have a heart for proclaiming the gospel to the many children the Lord has brought to us. They need space and a little wiggle room as well!

4. ***Increase our ability to offer our music worship to God.*** We believe that the proclamation of the true gospel of grace that is through faith alone is not only accomplished through preaching, but through our music worship. The gospel creates a yearning desire to sing and proclaim these truths *together* in grand music! We desire to offer to the Lord music with instruments and choirs and a facility design which allows us to lift the name of Christ in music to one another as commanded in Ephesians 5. Many church facilities today are acoustically designed more like a concert hall — with the focus being the stage. We desired a space more designed for the congregation to hear one another as well.

5. ***Increase our ability to fellowship with one another.*** Our facility did not have the space for our whole body to gather together in a fellowship event, such as a meal or receptions for events such as weddings and funerals. Yet the body life of the church is so vital to our interconnectedness and to fulfilling our mission to proclaim Christ to the world. With these fellowship opportunities, we not only cherish one another but we demonstrate our love for one another to those who are our guests. And by this love we have for one another, the lost will see the love of Christ which Jesus Himself said would be the sign to them that we belong to Christ.

6. ***Be more hospitable to our community.*** Our facility forced us to put our chairs so close to one another that it became awkward for guests. Our gracious members just got used to it, but that and other limitations of the facility created a sense of crowding and discomfort which could be avoided. Additionally, we desire to continue to reach out to the community through larger events, such as the Bible conference we host each year, and a facility with more

Appendix

reasonable accommodations would allow us to be more hospitable and welcoming.

7. *Fulfill our responsibility to the biblical gospel.* The gospel of Jesus Christ has continued to come under assault as countless false or at least weakened versions of the gospel are presented in churches across the land to unsuspecting souls who do not know they are being duped by an anemic plan of salvation. We are committed to the foundational pillars of the Reformation: salvation by grace alone through faith alone in Christ alone as revealed in the Scriptures alone to the glory of God alone. As such, it is our duty to maximize potential evangelistic opportunities via a facility which the community knows about and in which they would feel welcomed. While the disturbing Seeker Church movement seeks to use all external means possible to "attract" the lost without actually giving them a robust biblical gospel presentation, we conversely seek to be loving toward the lost so that we might have the privilege of calling them from darkness to the light of Christ. We believe that the Holy Spirit alone can save (John 3) and that no external means will bring people to salvation. But we are compelled to proclaim the gospel as the means by which the Holy Spirit regenerates the lost, since faith comes from hearing and hearing from the Word of Christ.

8. *Fulfill our responsibility to the life-changing impact of expository preaching.* The exposition of Scripture, allowing the Bible to speak for itself through a historical-grammatical hermeneutic (Bible study method), is the foundation of the health of the local church. Yet so few churches have engaged in the study and presentation of the Scriptures at a level which will challenge and mature the congregation to know Christ better and to understand the scope of the story

of redemptive history. Sadly, many believers are in church for decades without hearing an entire book of the Bible preached in an expositional manner which simply "exposes" (thus the term "expository") what the text actually says and means. As a church determined to be faithful to expository preaching, it is incumbent upon us to maximize potential impact to the best of our ability.

9. ***Devote a dedicated space to worship.*** While we see the wisdom of the classic "multi-purpose" room (which we have as of this writing), we also see the wisdom of a sacred space dedicated solely to the worship of God. As of this writing, we could not truly say our space is completely dedicated, partly because it is rented and is legally controlled by those *outside* the church. In Exodus 25, God told Israel to build a space dedicated *solely* to worship. God never said, "Go rent a warehouse from the Philistines."

10. ***Take advantage of a unique opportunity to leave a legacy.*** As I have traveled over the years and have had the opportunity to preach in different faithful churches, I am struck by some of the beautiful and functional church buildings which were built 25, 50, or even 100 years ago. My heart longs to travel back in time to the meetings those churches held so long ago to determine to give sacrificially to build those structures. I think about the older members who gave knowing they might not personally even see the finished result. Yet they were dedicated to the gospel of Christ and gave not for themselves but for those who would come after them. Giving to a capital campaign provides a unique opportunity to be that generation which blesses the next and which provides the very place from which the gospel will, Lord willing, be proclaimed until Christ returns.

Endnotes

1 John MacArthur, *Matthew 1–7 MacArthur New Testament Commentary* (Chicago, IL: Moody, 1985), 411.
2 "Prosperity Pastor Creflo Dollar: Abusing the Gospel," *Beginning and End*, June 26, 2012, accessed Feb 9, 2019, https://beginningandend.com/prosperity-pastor-creflo-dollar-abusing-the-gospel/.
3 A Greek-English Lexicon of the New Testament.
4 Ibid.
5 Exegetical Dictionary of the New Testament.
6 A Critical Lexicon and Concordance to the English and Greek New Testament.
7 Johannes P. Louw and Eugene Albert Nida, *Greek-English Lexicon of the New Testament: Based on Semantic Domains* (New York: United Bible Societies, 1996), 599.
8 Randy Alcorn, "Twelve Giving Stories," *Eternal Perspectives Ministries*, February 16, 2010, accessed Feb 9, 2019, https://www.epm.org/resources/2010/Feb/16/twelve-giving-stories/.
9 John MacArthur, "The Sheep's Responsibility," *Grace To You*, accessed January 2019, https://www.gty.org/library/sermons-library/52-25/the-sheeps-responsibility. This chapter contains numerous quotes from MacArthur. The chapter is derived from the message I originally preached the week after Dr. MacArthur celebrated his 50th anniversary as the pastor of Grace Community Church. Thus, the message served partially to honor the faithfulness of arguably the most prolific and impactful preacher since Charles Spurgeon.
10 Ibid.
11 Ibid.
12 Ibid.
13 John MacArthur, "The Shepherd's Responsibility," *Grace To You*, accessed January 2019, https://www.gty.org/library/sermons-library/52-24/the-shepherds-responsibility.

[14] Paul Ellingworth, *The Epistle to the Hebrews: A Commentary on the Greek Text*, New International Greek Testament Commentary (Grand Rapids, MI: Carlisle: W.B. Eerdmans; Paternoster Press, 1993), 641.

[15] Richard Cavendish, "Latimer and Ridley Burned at the Stake, *History Today*: 55:10, Oct 2005.

[16] https://en.wikipedia.org/wiki/List_of_Protestant_martyrs_of_the_English_Reformation, accessed January 2019. Although Wikipedia should not normally be considered a reliable resource for serious research, this particular compilation concerning protestant martyrs of the reformation contains almost 200 footnotes on sources consulted.

[17] To be fair, some independent churches have absolutely no problem pushing forward with grand facility plans. I am not characterizing all independent churches as having a problem with facility visions, but rather that they *can* have challenges in this area because of the some of the characteristics of an independent church. Much depends on the communication and leadership skills of the pastors and leadership as well.

[18] Jody Forehand, "Shouldn't a Church Look Like...," *Visioneering Studios*, August 4, 2014, accessed January 2019, http://www.visioneeringstudios.com/2014/08/shouldnt-a-church-look-like/.

[19] Eugene H. Merrill, *Everlasting Dominion: A Theology of the Old Testament* (Nashville, TN: B&H Publishing Group, 2006), 291.

[20] If you hold to differing ideas regarding the end times, that does not change the theological importance of giving because of God's kingdom. While true believers in Christ certainly often disagree about the order and nature of many end times events, there is broad agreement that the ultimate culmination of all things involves (a) the judgment of the unsaved, (b) the resurrection and glorification of the saved, and (c) the reign of God on a New Earth in a New Heaven.

[21] Matt Williams, "How Many Earths Can Fit in Jupiter?" *Universe Today*, May 28, 2010, accessed January 10, 2015, http://www.universetoday.com/65365/how-many-earths-can-fit-in-jupiter/.

www.ingramcontent.com/pod-product-compliance
Lightning Source LLC
Chambersburg PA
CBHW071956070426
42453CB00008BA/802